I0202005

www.itsmyfootprint.com

The Blessing Scriptures
© Copyright 2015 by Taka Sande

ISBN 978 0 620 69284 7

For permission requests, please contact the author directly at:
Taka Sande
Telephone: +27 72 324 2008
Fax: +27 (0) 86 602 5636
E-mail: admin@itsmyfootprint.com
Website: http://www.itsmyfootprint.com/
Postal: Postnet Suite 35, Private Bag X592, Silverton 0127, South Africa. Cover

Design by: Takudzwanashe Kucherera

www.itsmyfootprint.com

Table of Contents

www.itsmyfootprint.com

The Power Of The Word

The Word of God is the most powerful force in the world, as a child of God it is important to unlock this power by applying the Word of God consistently in all situations. We unlock the power of the Word by believing in the Word, delighting in the Word, studying the Word and confessing the Word.

On the other hand we often battle to find where to start from when reading the Bible and we struggle to maintain a constant devotional life. This is how this book will help you. It has verses that benefits your immediately. The scriptures will relate to your personal life. And as you meditate on them they will speak to you directly.

The idea of this book is to have a collection of scriptures that will fire up your life, and give you daily motivation to enjoy everyday life and fulfill your dreams. Few scriptures a day will help you maintain a positive mind throughout the day. They will energize your to get out of bed to fulfil your calling with a purpose.

Are you going through a rough time and facing huge challenges? This collection of scripture will surely speak to your situation and empower you by giving you a new outlook to your future so that you can face your challenges and overcome them.

Applying the rich collection of scriptures in this book will change your life. Read each verse with a calm mind, memorize them, recite them loudly and share them to your family and friends!

1
Blessing

Genesis 1:28 And God blessed them, and God said to them, Be fruitful, and multiply, and replenish the earth, and subdue it: and have dominion over the fish of the sea, and over the fowl of the air, and over every living thing that moves on the earth. (AKJV)

Genesis 9:1 And God blessed Noah and his sons, and said to them, Be fruitful, and multiply, and replenish the earth. (AKJV)

Genesis 9:7 And you, be you fruitful, and multiply; bring forth abundantly in the earth, and multiply therein. (AKJV)

Genesis 12:1-3 Now the LORD had said to Abram, Get you out of your country, and from your kindred, and from your father's house, to a land that I will show you: And I will make of you a great nation, and I will bless you, and make your name great; and you shall be a blessing: And I will bless them that bless you, and curse him that curses you: and in you shall all families of the earth be blessed. (AKJV)

Genesis 17:1-2 And when Abram was ninety years old and nine, the LORD appeared to Abram, and said to him, I am the Almighty God; walk before me, and be you perfect. And I will make my covenant between me and you, and will multiply you exceedingly. (AKJV)

Genesis 26:12 Then Isaac sowed in that land, and received in the same year an hundred times: and the LORD blessed him. (AKJV)

Joshua 1:3 Every place that the sole of your foot shall tread on, that have I given to you, as I said to Moses. (AKJV)

Deuteronomy 15:10-11 You shall surely give him, and your heart shall not be grieved when you give to him: because that for this thing the LORD your God shall bless you in all your works, and in all that you put your hand to. For the poor shall never cease out of the land: therefore I command you, saying, You shall open your hand wide to your brother, to your poor, and to your needy, in your land. (AKJV)

Deuteronomy 28:3-6 Blessed shall you be in the city, and blessed shall you be in the field. Blessed shall be the fruit of your body, and the fruit of your ground, and the fruit of your cattle, the increase of your cows, and the flocks of your sheep. Blessed shall be your basket and your store. Blessed shall you be when you come in, and blessed shall you be when you go out. (AKJV)

Deuteronomy 28:7-10 The LORD shall cause your enemies that rise up against you to be smitten before your face: they shall come out against you one way, and flee before you seven ways. The LORD shall command the blessing on you in your storehouses, and in all that you set your hand to; and he shall bless you in the land which the LORD your God gives you. The LORD shall establish you an holy people to himself, as he has sworn to you, if you shall keep the commandments of the LORD your God, and walk in his ways. And all people of the earth shall see that you are called by the name of the LORD; and they shall be afraid of you. (AKJV)

Ecclesiastes 10:19 A feast is made for laughter, and wine makes merry: but money answers all things. (AKJV)

Deuteronomy 28:11-14 And the LORD shall make you plenteous in goods, in the fruit of your body, and in the fruit of your cattle, and in the fruit of your ground, in the land which the LORD swore to your fathers to give you. The LORD shall open to you his good treasure, the heaven to give the rain to your land in his season, and to bless all the work of your hand: and you shall lend to many nations, and you shall not borrow. And the LORD shall make you the head, and not the tail; and you shall be above only, and you shall not be beneath; if that you listen to the commandments of the LORD your God, which I command you this day, to observe and to do them: And you shall not go aside from any of the words which I command you this day, to the right hand, or to the left, to go after other gods to serve them. (AKJV)

Deuteronomy 30:9-10 And the LORD your God will make you plenteous in every work of your hand, in the fruit of your body, and in the fruit of your cattle, and in the fruit of your land, for good: for the LORD will again rejoice over you for good, as he rejoiced over your fathers: If you shall listen to the voice of the LORD your God, to keep his commandments and his statutes which are written in this book of the law, and if you turn to the LORD your God with all your heart, and with all your soul. (AKJV)

Deuteronomy 30:19-20 I call heaven and earth to record this day against you, that I have set before you life and death, blessing and cursing: therefore choose life, that both you and your seed may live: That you may love the LORD your God, and that you may obey his voice, and that you may hold to him: for he is your life, and the length of your days: that you may dwell in the land which the LORD swore to your fathers, to Abraham, to Isaac, and to Jacob, to give them. (AKJV)

www.itsmyfootprint.com

1 Chronicles 29:10-13 Why David blessed the LORD before all the congregation: and David said, Blessed be you, LORD God of Israel our father, for ever and ever. Yours, O LORD is the greatness, and the power, and the glory, and the victory, and the majesty: for all that is in the heaven and in the earth is yours; your is the kingdom, O LORD, and you are exalted as head above all. Both riches and honor come of you, and you reign over all; and in your hand is power and might; and in your hand it is to make great, and to give strength to all. Now therefore, our God, we thank you, and praise your glorious name. (AKJV)

Psalm 1:1-6 Blessed is the man who walks not in the counsel of the ungodly, nor stands in the path of sinners, nor sits in the seat of the scornful; but his delight is in the law of the Lord, and in His law he meditates day and night. He shall be like a tree planted by the rivers of water, that brings forth its fruit in its season, whose leaf also shall not wither; and whatever he does shall prosper. The ungodly are not so, but are like the chaff which the wind drives away. Therefore the ungodly shall not stand in the judgment, nor sinners in the congregation of the righteous. For the Lord knows the way of the righteous, but the way of the ungodly shall perish. (AKJV)

Proverbs 21:20 There are precious treasures and oil in the dwelling of the wise, but a self-confident {and} foolish man swallows it up {and} wastes it. AMP

Proverbs 29:18 Where there is no vision, the people perish: but he that keepeth the law, happy is he. (AKJV)

Ecclesiastes 11:1-2 Cast your bread on the waters: for you shall find it after many days. Give a portion to seven, and also to eight; for you know not what evil shall be on the earth. (AKJV)

Isaiah 45:3 And I will give you the treasures of darkness, and hidden riches of secret places, that you may know that I, the LORD, which call you by your name, am the God of Israel. (AKJV)

Haggai 2:8 The silver is Mine and the gold is Mine, says the Lord of hosts. AMP

Malachi 3:10-12 Bring you all the tithes into the storehouse, that there may be meat in my house, and prove me now herewith, said the LORD of hosts, if I will not open you the windows of heaven, and pour you out a blessing, that there shall not be room enough to receive it. And I will rebuke the devourer for your sakes, and he shall not destroy the fruits of your ground; neither shall your vine cast her fruit before the time in the field, said the LORD of hosts. And all nations shall call you blessed: for you shall be a delightsome land, said the LORD of hosts. (AKJV)

Matthew 6:2-4 Thus, whenever you give to the poor, do not blow a trumpet before you, as the hypocrites in the synagogues and in the streets like to do, that they may be recognized {and} honored {and} praised by men. Truly I tell you, they have their reward in full already. But when you give to charity, do not let your left hand know what your right hand is doing, So that your deeds of charity may be in secret; and your Father Who sees in secret will reward you {openly.} (AMP)

Matthew 6:19-21 Do not gather {and} heap up {and} store up for yourselves treasures on earth, where moth and rust {and} worm consume {and} destroy, and where thieves break through and steal. But gather {and} heap up {and} store for yourselves treasures in heaven, where neither moth nor rust {nor} worm consume {and} destroy, and where thieves do not break through and steal; For where your treasure is, there will your heart be also (AMP).

Matthew 7:7-8 Keep on asking and it will be given you; keep on seeking and you will find; keep on knocking [reverently] and [the door] will be opened to you. For everyone who keeps on asking receives; and he who keeps on seeking finds; and to him who keeps on knocking, [the door] will be opened. (AMP)

John 15:7 If you live in Me [abide vitally united to Me] and My words remain in you {and} continue to live in your hearts, ask whatever you will, and it shall be done for you. (AMP)

2 Corinthians 10:3-5 For though we walk (live) in the flesh, we are not carrying on our warfare according to the flesh {and} using mere human weapons. For the weapons of our warfare are not physical [weapons of flesh and blood], but they are mighty before God for the overthrow and destruction of strongholds, [inasmuch as we] refute arguments and theories and reasonings and every proud and lofty thing that sets itself up against the [true] knowledge of God; and we lead every thought and purpose away captive into the obedience of Christ (the Messiah, the Anointed One). (AMP)

Amos 9:13 Behold, the days come, said the LORD, that the plowman shall overtake the reaper, and the treader of grapes him that sows seed; and the mountains shall drop sweet wine, and all the hills shall melt. (AKJV)

3 John 1:2 Beloved, I pray that you may prosper in every way and [that your body] may keep well, even as [I know] your soul keeps well {and} prospers. (AMP)

Mark 10:29-31 Jesus said, Truly I tell you, there is no one who has given up {and} left house or brothers or sisters or mother or father or children or lands for My sake and for the Gospel's. Who will not receive a hundred times as much now in this time--houses and brothers and sisters and mothers and children and lands, with persecutions--and in the age to come, eternal life. But many [who are now] first will be last [then], and many [who are now] last will be first [then]. (AMP)

Luke 18:29-30 And He said to them, I say to you truly, there is no one who has left house or wife or brothers or parents or children for the sake of the kingdom of God Who will not receive in return many times more in this world and, in the coming age, eternal life. (AMP)

2

Business and

Finance

Romans 13:8 Keep out of debt {and} owe no man anything, except to love one another; for he who loves his neighbor [who practices loving others] has fulfilled the Law [relating to one's fellowmen, meeting all its requirements]. (AMP)

1 Timothy 6:10 For the love of money is a root of all evils; it is through this craving that some have been led astray {and} have wandered from the faith and pierced themselves through with many acute [mental] pangs. (AMP)

Luke 14:28-30 For which of you, wishing to build a farm building, does not first sit down and calculate the cost [to see] whether he has sufficient means to finish it? Otherwise, when he has laid the foundation and is unable to complete [the building], all who see it will begin to mock {and} jeer at him, Saying, This man began to build and was not able (worth enough) to finish. (AMP)

Ephesians 6:9 YOU MASTERS, act on the same [principle] toward them and give up threatening {and} using violent {and} abusive words, knowing that He Who is both their Master and yours is in heaven, and that there is no respect of persons (no partiality) with Him. (AMP)

Matthew 25:14-30 His master said to him, Well done, you upright (honorable, admirable) and faithful servant! You have been faithful {and} trustworthy over a little; I will put you in charge of much. Enter into {and} share the joy (the delight, the blessedness) which your master enjoys. (AMP)

Colossians 3:22 Servants, obey in everything those who are your earthly masters, not only when their eyes are on you as pleasers of men, but in simplicity of purpose [with all your heart] because of your reverence for the Lord {and} as a sincere expression of your devotion to Him. Whatever may be your task, work at it heartily (from the soul), as [something done] for the Lord and not for men, Knowing [with all certainty] that it is from the Lord [and not from men] that you will receive the inheritance which is your [real] reward. [The One Whom] you are actually serving [is] the Lord Christ (the Messiah). (AMP)

Genesis 39:2 And the LORD was with Joseph, and he was a prosperous man; and he was in the house of his master the Egyptian. (AKJV)

3
Desire

Philippians 4:19 But my God shall supply all your need according to his riches in glory by Christ Jesus. (AMP)

1 John 2:15-17 Do not love {or} cherish the world or the things that are in the world. If anyone loves the world, love for the Father is not in him. For all that is in the world--the lust of the flesh [craving for sensual gratification] and the lust of the eyes [greedy longings of the mind] and the pride of life [assurance in one's own resources or in the stability of earthly things]--these do not come from the Father but are from the world [itself]. And the world passes away {and} disappears, and with it the forbidden cravings (the passionate desires, the lust) of it; but he who does the will of God and carries out His purposes in his life abides (remains) forever. (AMP)

4

Faith and Hope

Romans 5:5 Now hope does not disappoint, because the love of God has been poured out in our hearts by the Holy Spirit who was given to us (NKJV).

2 Corinthians 4:18 Since we consider {and} look not to the things that are seen but to the things that are unseen; for the things that are visible are temporal (brief and fleeting), but the things that are invisible are deathless {and} everlasting. (AMP)

Galatians 3:6-7 Thus Abraham believed in {and} adhered to {and} trusted in {and} relied on God, and it was reckoned {and} placed to his account {and} credited as righteousness (as conformity to the divine will in purpose, thought, and action). Know {and} understand that it is [really] the people [who live] by faith who are [the true] sons of Abraham. (AMP)

1 Thessalonians 5:24 Faithful is He Who is calling you [to Himself] {and} utterly trustworthy, and He will also do it [fulfill His call by hallowing and keeping you]. (AMP)

Hebrews 10:23 So let us seize and hold fast and retain without wavering the hope we cherish and confess and our acknowledgement of it, for He Who promised is reliable (sure) and faithful to His word. (AMP)

Hebrews 11:1 NOW FAITH is the assurance (the confirmation, the title deed) of the things [we] hope for, being the proof of things [we] do not see {and} the conviction of their reality [faith perceiving as real fact what is not revealed to the senses]. (AMP)

Hebrews 11:6 But without faith it is impossible to please {and} be satisfactory to Him. For whoever would come near to God must [necessarily] believe that God exists and that He is the rewarder of those who earnestly {and} diligently seek Him [out]. (AMP)

Matthew 8:8-13 But the centurion replied to Him, Lord, I am not worthy {or} fit to have You come under my roof; but only speak the word, and my servant boy will be cured. For I also am a man subject to authority, with soldiers subject to me. And I say to one, Go, and he goes; and to another, Come, and he comes; and to my slave, Do this, and he does it. When Jesus heard him, He marveled and said to those who followed Him [who adhered steadfastly to Him, conforming to His example in living and, if need be, in dying also], I tell you truly, I have not found so much faith as this with anyone, even in Israel. I tell you, many will come from east and west, and will sit at table with Abraham, Isaac, and Jacob in the kingdom of heaven, While the sons {and} heirs of the kingdom will be driven out into the darkness outside, where there will be weeping and grinding of teeth. Then to the centurion Jesus said, Go; it shall be done for you as you have believed. And the servant boy was restored to health at that very moment. (AMP)

Mark 9:23 Jesus said to him, "If you can believe, all things are possible to him who believes" (NKJV).

John 12:15 Do not fear, O Daughter of Zion! Look! Your King is coming, sitting on a donkey's colt! [Zech. 9:9.] (AMP)

Matthew 17:20 He said to them, Because of the littleness of your faith [that is, your lack of firmly relying trust]. For truly I say to you, if you have faith [that is living] like a grain of mustard seed, you can say to this mountain, Move from here to yonder place, and it will move; and nothing will be impossible to you. (AMP)

Matthew 18:19-20 Again I tell you, if two of you on earth agree (harmonize together, make a symphony together) about whatever [anything and everything] they may ask, it will come to pass {and} be done for them by My Father in heaven. For wherever two or three are gathered (drawn together as My followers) in (into) My name, there I AM in the midst of them. (AMP)

Matthew 21:21-22 And Jesus answered them, Truly I say to you, if you have faith (a firm relying trust) and do not doubt, you will not only do what has been done to the fig tree, but even if you say to this mountain, Be taken up and cast into the sea, it will be done. And whatever you ask for in prayer, having faith {and} [really] believing, you will receive. (AMP)

5
Faithfulness

Romans 4:18-22 [For Abraham, human reason for] hope being gone, hoped in faith that he should become the father of many nations, as he had been promised, So [numberless] shall your descendants be. He did not weaken in faith when he considered the [utter] impotence of his own body, which was as good as dead because he was about a hundred years old, or [when he considered] the barrenness of Sarah's [deadened] womb. No unbelief {or} distrust made him waver (doubtingly question) concerning the promise of God, but he grew strong {and} was empowered by faith as he gave praise {and} glory to God, Fully satisfied {and} assured that God was able {and} mighty to keep His word {and} to do what He had promised. That is why his faith was credited to him as righteousness (right standing with God). (AMP)

1 Kings 2:2-3 I go the way of all the earth: be you strong therefore, and show yourself a man; And keep the charge of the LORD your God, to walk in his ways, to keep his statutes, and his commandments, and his judgments, and his testimonies, as it is written in the law of Moses, that you may prosper in all that you do, and wherever you turn yourself: (AKJV)

Job 17:9 The righteous also shall hold on his way, and he that has clean hands shall be stronger and stronger. (AKJV)

Psalm 31:23 O love the Lord, all you His saints! The Lord preserves the faithful, and plentifully pays back him who deals haughtily. (AMP)

Luke 16:10-12 He who is faithful in a very little [thing] is faithful also in much, and he who is dishonest {and} unjust in a very little [thing] is dishonest {and} unjust also in much. Therefore if you have not been faithful in the [case of] unrighteous mammon (deceitful riches, money, possessions), who will entrust to you the true riches? And if you have not proved faithful in that which belongs to another [whether God or man], who will give you that which is your own [that is, the true riches]? (AMP)

Proverbs 28:20 A faithful man shall abound with blessings: but he that makes haste to be rich shall not be innocent. (AKJV)

Matthew 24:45-47 Who then is the faithful, thoughtful, {and} wise servant, whom his master has put in charge of his household to give to the others the food {and} supplies at the proper time? Blessed (happy, fortunate, and to be envied) is that servant whom, when his master comes, he will find so doing. I solemnly declare to you, he will set him over all his possessions.

6
Family

1 Corinthians 7:14 Now concerning the things of which you wrote to me: It is good for a man not to touch a woman. Nevertheless, because of sexual immorality, let each man have his own wife, and let each woman have her own husband. Let the husband render to his wife the affection due her, and likewise also the wife to her husband. The wife does not have authority over her own body, but the husband does. And likewise the husband does not have authority over his own body, but the wife does (NKJV).

Proverbs 18:22 Whoever finds a wife finds a good thing, and obtains favor of the LORD. (AKJV)

Ephesians 6:1 CHILDREN, OBEY your parents in the Lord [as His representatives], for this is just and right. Honor (esteem and value as precious) your father and your mother--this is the first commandment with a promise. That all may be well with you and that you may live long on the earth. (AMP)

Ephesians 5:25-29 HUSBANDS, love your wives, as Christ loved the church and gave Himself up for her, So that He might sanctify her, having cleansed her by the washing of water with the Word, That He might present the church to Himself in glorious splendor, without spot or wrinkle or any such things [that she might be holy and faultless]. Even so husbands should love their wives as [being in a sense] their own bodies. He who loves his own wife loves himself. For no man ever hated his own flesh, but nourishes {and} carefully protects and cherishes it, as Christ does the church, (AMP)

Ephesians 5:31-33 FOR THIS REASON a man shall leave his father and his mother and shall be joined to his wife, and the two shall become one flesh. This mystery is very great, but I speak concerning [the relation of] Christ and the church. However, let each man of you [without exception] love his wife as [being in a sense] his very own self; and let the wife see that she respects {and} reverences her husband [that she notices him, regards him, honors him, prefers him, venerates, and esteems him; and that she defers to him, praises him, and loves and admires him exceedingly]. [I Peter. 3:2.] (AMP)

Ephesians 6:1-3 CHILDREN, OBEY your parents in the Lord [as His representatives], for this is just and right. Honor (esteem and value as precious) your father and your mother--this is the first commandment with a promise- That all may be well with you and that you may live long on the earth. (AMP)

Ephesians 6:4 FATHERS, do not irritate {and} provoke your children to anger [do not exasperate them to resentment], but rear them [tenderly] in the training {and} discipline and the counsel {and} admonition of the Lord. (AMP)

Ephesians 5:22-24 Wives, be subject (be submissive and adapt yourselves) to your own husbands as [a service] to the Lord. For the husband is head of the wife as Christ is the Head of the church, Himself the Savior of [His] body. As the church is subject to Christ, so let wives also be subject in everything to their husbands. (AMP)

7
Forgiveness

Galatians 3:11 Now it is evident that no person is justified (declared righteous and brought into right standing with God) through the Law, for the Scripture says, The man in right standing with God [the just, the righteous] shall live by {and} out of faith {and} he who through {and} by faith is declared righteous {and} in right standing with God shall live. (AMP)

Ephesians 3:12 In Whom, because of our faith in Him, we dare to have the boldness (courage and confidence) of free access (an unreserved approach to God with freedom and without fear). (AMP)

Ephesians 2:13-15 But now in Christ Jesus, you who once were [so] far away, through (by, in) the blood of Christ have been brought near. For He is [Himself] our peace (our bond of unity and harmony). He has made us both [Jew and Gentile] one [body], and has broken down (destroyed, abolished) the hostile dividing wall between us, By abolishing in His [own crucified] flesh the enmity [caused by] the Law with its decrees and ordinances [which He annulled]; that He from the two might create in Himself one new man [one new quality of humanity out of the two], so making peace. (AMP)

James 5:15 And the prayer [that is] of faith will save him who is sick, and the Lord will restore him; and if he has committed sins, he will be forgiven. (AMP)

Psalm 103:2-3 Bless (affectionately, gratefully praise) the Lord, O my soul, and forget not [one of] all His benefits—Who forgives [every one of] all your iniquities, Who heals [each one of] all your diseases (AMP).

2 Chronicles 7:14 If my people, which are called by my name, shall humble themselves, and pray, and seek my face, and turn from their wicked ways; then will I hear from heaven, and will forgive their sin, and will heal their land. (AKJV)

1 John 1:9 If we [freely] admit that we have sinned and confess our sins, He is faithful and just (true to His own nature and promises) and will forgive our sins [dismiss our lawlessness] and [continuously] cleanse us from all unrighteousness [everything not in conformity to His will in purpose, thought, and action]. (AMP)

Mark 11:22-26 And Jesus, replying, said to them, Have faith in God [constantly] Truly I tell you, whoever says to this mountain, Be lifted up and thrown into the sea! and does not doubt at all in his heart but believes that what he says will take place, it will be done for him. For this reason I am telling you, whatever you ask for in prayer, believe (trust and be confident) that it is granted to you, and you will [get it]. And whenever you stand praying, if you have anything against anyone, forgive him {and} let it drop (leave it, let it go), in order that your Father Who is in heaven may also forgive you your [own] failings {and} shortcomings {and} let them drop.
{But if you do not forgive, neither will your Father in heaven forgive your failings and shortcomings.} (AMP)

Ephesians 2:11-12 Therefore, remember that at one time you were Gentiles (heathens) in the flesh, called Uncircumcision by those who called themselves Circumcision, [itself a mere mark] in the flesh made by human hands. [Remember] that you were at that time separated (living apart) from Christ [excluded from all part in Him], utterly estranged {and} outlawed from the rights of Israel as a nation, and strangers with no share in the sacred compacts of the [Messianic] promise [with no knowledge of or right in God's agreements, His covenants]. And you had no hope (no promise); you were in the world without God. (AMP)

8
Freedom & Deliverance

www.itsmyfootprint.com

James 5:13-16 Is anyone among you afflicted (ill-treated, suffering evil)? He should pray. Is anyone glad at heart? He should sing praise [to God].Is anyone among you sick? He should call in the church elders (the spiritual guides). And they should pray over him, anointing him with oil in the Lord's name. And the prayer [that is] of faith will save him who is sick, and the Lord will restore him; and if he has committed sins, he will be forgiven. Confess to one another therefore your faults (your slips, your false steps, your offenses, your sins) and pray [also] for one another, that you may be healed {and} restored [to a spiritual tone of mind and heart]. The earnest (heartfelt, continued) prayer of a righteous man makes tremendous power available [dynamic in its working]. (AMP)

Matthew 16:25-26 For whoever is bent on saving his [temporal] life [his comfort and security here] shall lose it [eternal life]; and whoever loses his life [his comfort and security here] for My sake shall find it [life everlasting]. For what will it profit a man if he gains the whole world and forfeits his life [his blessed life in the kingdom of God]? Or what would a man give as an exchange for his [blessed] life [in the kingdom of God]? (AMP)

Romans 5:1 Therefore, since we are justified (acquitted, declared righteous, and given a right standing with God) through faith, let us [grasp the fact that we] have [the peace of reconciliation to hold and to enjoy] peace with God through our Lord Jesus Christ (the Messiah, the Anointed One). (AMP)

2 Corinthians 5:17 Therefore, if anyone is in Christ, he is a new creation; old things have passed away; behold, all things have become new (NKJV).

1 John 3:8 [But] he who commits sin [who practices evildoing] is of the devil [takes his character from the evil one], for the devil has sinned (violated the divine law) from the beginning. The reason the Son of God was made manifest (visible) was to undo (destroy, loosen, and dissolve) the works the devil [has done]. (AMP)

Joshua 21:43-45 And the LORD gave to Israel all the land which he swore to give to their fathers; and they possessed it, and dwelled therein. And the LORD gave them rest round about, according to all that he swore to their fathers: and there stood not a man of all their enemies before them; the LORD delivered all their enemies into their hand. There failed not ought of any good thing which the LORD had spoken to the house of Israel; all came to pass. (AKJV)

Psalm 34:19-20 Many are the afflictions of the righteous: but the LORD delivers him out of them all. He keeps all his bones: not one of them is broken. (AKJV)

Psalm 91:10-15 There shall no evil befall you, neither shall any plague come near your dwelling. For he shall give his angels charge over you, to keep you in all your ways. They shall bear you up in their hands, lest you dash your foot against a stone. You shall tread on the lion and adder: the young lion and the dragon shall you trample under feet. Because he has set his love on me, therefore will I deliver him: I will set him on high, because he has known my name. He shall call on me, and I will answer him: I will be with him in trouble; I will deliver him, and honor him. (AKJV)

www.itsmyfootprint.com

Isaiah 35:3-4 Strengthen you the weak hands, and confirm the feeble knees. Say to them that are of a fearful heart, Be strong, fear not: behold, your God will come with vengeance, even God with a recompense; he will come and save you. (AKJV)

Isaiah 54:13-17 "All your children shall be taught by the Lord, and great shall be the peace of your children. In righteousness you shall be established; you shall be far from oppression, for you shall not fear; and from terror, for it shall not come near you. Indeed they shall surely assemble, but not because of Me. Whoever assembles against you shall fall for your sake. Behold, I have created the blacksmith who blows the coals in the fire, who brings forth an instrument for his work; and I have created the spoiler to destroy. No weapon formed against you shall prosper, and every tongue which rises against you in judgment you shall condemn. This is the heritage of the servants of the Lord, and their righteousness is from Me," says the Lord. (AKJV)

Isaiah 58:8 Then shall your light break forth as the morning, and your health shall spring forth speedily: and your righteousness shall go before you; the glory of the LORD shall be your rear guard. (AKJV)

1 Corinthians 1:18 For the story {and} message of the cross is sheer absurdity {and} folly to those who are perishing {and} on their way to perdition, but to us who are being saved it is the [manifestation of] the power of God. (AMP)

Revelation 12:11 And they have overcome (conquered) him by means of the blood of the Lamb and by the utterance of their testimony, for they did not love {and} cling to life even when faced with death [holding their lives cheap till they had to die for their witnessing]. (AMP)

James 4:7-8 So be subject to God. Resist the devil [stand firm against him], and he will flee from you. Come close to God and He will come close to you. [Recognize that you are] sinners, get your soiled hands clean; [realize that you have been disloyal] wavering individuals with divided interests, and purify your hearts [of your spiritual adultery]. (AMP)

1 Peter 1:18-19 You must know (recognize) that you were redeemed (ransomed) from the useless (fruitless) way of living inherited by tradition from [your] forefathers, not with corruptible things [such as] silver and gold, But [you were purchased] with the precious blood of Christ (the Messiah), like that of a [sacrificial] lamb without blemish or spot. (AMP)

9
Giving & Charity

Proverbs 19:17 He that has pity on the poor lends to the LORD; and that which he has given will he pay him again. (AKJV)

Matthew 10:40-42 He who receives {and} welcomes {and} accepts you receives {and} welcomes {and} accepts Me, and he who receives {and} welcomes {and} accepts Me receives {and} welcomes {and} accepts Him Who sent Me. He who receives {and} welcomes {and} accepts a prophet because he is a prophet shall receive a prophet's reward, and he who receives {and} welcomes {and} accepts a righteous man because he is a righteous man shall receive a righteous man's reward. And whoever gives to one of these little ones [in rank or influence] even a cup of cold water because he is My disciple, surely I declare to you, he shall not lose his reward. (AMP)

Romans 12:13-16 Contribute to the needs of God's people [sharing in the necessities of the saints]; pursue the practice of hospitality. Bless those who persecute you [who are cruel in their attitude toward you]; bless and do not curse them. Rejoice with those who rejoice [sharing others' joy], and weep with those who weep [sharing others' grief]. Live in harmony with one another; do not be haughty (snobbish, high-minded, exclusive), but readily adjust yourself to [people, things] {and} give yourselves to humble tasks. Never overestimate yourself {or} be wise in your own conceits. (AMP)

Acts 20:35 ...being mindful of the words of the Lord Jesus, how He Himself said, It is more blessed (makes one happier and more to be envied) to give than to receive. (AMP)

Galatians 6:7-10 Do not be deceived {and} deluded {and} misled; God will not allow Himself to be sneered at (scorned, disdained, or mocked by mere pretensions or professions, or by His precepts being set aside.) [He inevitably deludes himself who attempts to delude God.] For whatever a man sows, that {and} that only is what he will reap. For he who sows to his own flesh (lower nature, sensuality) will from the flesh reap decay {and} ruin {and} destruction, but he who sows to the Spirit will from the Spirit reap eternal life. And let us not lose heart {and} grow weary {and} faint in acting nobly {and} doing right, for in due time {and} at the appointed season we shall reap, if we do not loosen {and} relax our courage {and} faint. So then, as occasion {and} opportunity open up to us, let us do good [morally] to all people [not only being useful or profitable to them, but also doing what is for their spiritual good and advantage]. Be mindful to be a blessing, especially to those of the household of faith [those who belong to God's family with you, the believers]. (AMP)

Acts 4:34 Nor was there a destitute {or} needy person among them, for as many as were owners of lands or houses proceeded to sell them, and one by one they brought (gave back) the amount received from the sales. (AMP)

Galatians 6:10 So then, as occasion {and} opportunity open up to us, let us do good [morally] to all people [not only being useful or profitable to them, but also doing what is for their spiritual good and advantage]. Be mindful to be a blessing, especially to those of the household of faith [those who belong to God's family with you, the believers]. (AMP)

Matthew 7:11 If you then, evil as you are, know how to give good {and} advantageous gifts to your children, how much more will your Father Who is in heaven [perfect as He is] give good {and} advantageous things to those who keep on asking Him! (AMP)

Ecclesiastes 11:6 In the morning sow your seed, and in the evening withhold not your hand: for you know not whether shall prosper, either this or that, or whether they both shall be alike good. (AKJV)

Luke 6:38 Give, and [gifts] will be given to you; good measure, pressed down, shaken together, and running over, will they pour into [the pouch formed by] the bosom [of your robe and used as a bag]. For with the measure you deal out [with the measure you use when you confer benefits on others], it will be measured back to you. (AMP)

2 Corinthians 9:6 [Remember] this: he who sows sparingly {and} grudgingly will also reap sparingly {and} grudgingly, and he who sows generously [that blessings may come to someone] will also reap generously {and} with blessings. (AMP)

2 Corinthians 9:10-11 And [God] Who provides seed for the sower and bread for eating will also provide and multiply your [resources for] sowing and increase the fruits of your righteousness [which manifests itself in active goodness, kindness, and charity]. Thus you will be enriched in all things {and} in every way, so that you can be generous, and [your generosity as it is] administered by us will bring forth thanksgiving to God. (AMP)

www.itsmyfootprint.com

Galatians 6:7-9 Do not be deceived {and} deluded {and} misled; God will not allow Himself to be sneered at (scorned, disdained, or mocked by mere pretensions or professions, or by His precepts being set aside.) [He inevitably deludes himself who attempts   to delude God.] For whatever a man sows, that {and} that only   is what he will reap. For he who sows to his own flesh (lower nature, sensuality) will from the flesh reap decay {and} ruin {and} destruction, but he who sows to the Spirit will from the Spirit reap eternal life. And let us not lose heart {and} grow weary {and} faint in acting nobly {and} doing right, for in due time {and} at the appointed season we shall reap, if we do not loosen {and} relax our courage {and} faint. (AMP)

10
God's Power

Genesis 18:19 For I know him, that he will command his children and his household after him, and they shall keep the way of the LORD, to do justice and judgment; that the LORD may bring on Abraham that which he has spoken of him. (AKJV)

Leviticus 26:1-26 You shall make you no idols nor graven image, neither raise you up a standing image, neither shall you set up any image of stone in your land, to bow down to it: for I am the LORD your God. You shall keep my sabbaths, and reverence my sanctuary: I am the LORD. If you walk in my statutes, and keep my commandments, and do them; Then I will give you rain in due season, and the land shall yield her increase, and the trees of the field shall yield their fruit. And your threshing shall reach to the vintage, and the vintage shall reach to the sowing time: and you shall eat your bread to the full, and dwell in your land safely. And I will give peace in the land, and you shall lie down, and none shall make you afraid: and I will rid evil beasts out of the land, neither shall the sword go through your land. And you shall chase your enemies, and they shall fall before you by the sword. And five of you shall chase a hundred, and a hundred of you shall put ten thousand to flight: and your enemies shall fall before you by the sword. For I will have respect to you, and make you fruitful, and multiply you, and establish my covenant with you. And you shall eat old store, and bring forth the old because of the new. And I set my tabernacle among you: and my soul shall not abhor you. And I will walk among you, and will be your God, and you shall be my people. I am the LORD your God, which brought you forth out of the land of Egypt, that you should not be their slaves; and I have broken the bands of your yoke, and made you go upright. (AKJV)

Leviticus 27:30 And all the tithe of the land, whether of the seed of the land or of the fruit of the tree, is the Lord's; it is holy to the Lord. AMP

Numbers 23:19 God is not a man, that he should lie; neither the son of man, that he should repent: has he said, and shall he not do it? or has he spoken, and shall he not make it good? (AKJV)

Exodus 12:13 And the blood shall be to you for a token upon the houses where ye are: and when I see the blood, I will pass over you, and the plague shall not be upon you to destroy you…. (AKJV)

Exodus 15:2 The LORD is my strength and song, and he is become my salvation: he is my God, and I will prepare him an habitation; my father's God, and I will exalt him. (AKJV)

Exodus 20:1-3 And God spoke all these words, saying, I am the LORD your God, which have brought you out of the land of Egypt, out of the house of bondage. You shall have no other gods before me. (AKJV)

Deuteronomy 5:33 You shall walk in all the ways which the LORD your God has commanded you, that you may live, and that it may be well with you, and that you may prolong your days in the land which you shall possess. (AKJV)

Psalm 24:1 The earth is the LORD's, and the fullness thereof; the world, and they that dwell therein. (AKJV)

Deuteronomy 6:1-5 Now these are the commandments, the statutes, and the judgments, which the LORD your God commanded to teach you, that you might do them in the land where you go to possess it: That you might fear the LORD your God, to keep all his statutes and his commandments, which I command you, you, and your son, and your son's son, all the days of your life; and that your days may be prolonged. Hear therefore, O Israel, and observe to do it; that it may be well with you, and that you may increase mightily, as the LORD God of your fathers has promised you, in the land that flows with milk and honey. Hear, O Israel: The LORD our God is one LORD: And you shall love the LORD your God with all your heart, and with all your soul, and with all your might. (AKJV)

Deuteronomy 7:9-15 Know therefore that the LORD your God, he is God, the faithful God, which keeps covenant and mercy with them that love him and keep his commandments to a thousand generations; And repays them that hate him to their face, to destroy them: he will not be slack to him that hates him, he will repay him to his face. You shall therefore keep the commandments, and the statutes, and the judgments, which I command you this day, to do them. Why it shall come to pass, if you listen to these judgments, and keep, and do them, that the LORD your God shall keep to you the covenant and the mercy which he swore to your fathers: And he will love you, and bless you, and multiply you: he will also bless the fruit of your womb, and the fruit of your land, your corn, and your wine, and your oil, the increase of your cows, and the flocks of your sheep, in the land which he swore to your fathers to give you. You shall be blessed above all people: there shall not be male or female barren among you, or among your cattle. And the LORD will take away from you all sickness, and will put none of the evil diseases of Egypt, which you know, on you; but will lay them on all them that hate you. (AKJV)

www.itsmyfootprint.com

Deuteronomy 9:3 Understand therefore this day, that the LORD your God is he which goes over before you; as a consuming fire he shall destroy them, and he shall bring them down before your face: (AKJV)

Deuteronomy 16:15 Seven days shall you keep a solemn feast to the LORD your God in the place which the LORD shall choose: because the LORD your God shall bless you in all your increase, and in all the works of your hands, therefore you shall surely rejoice. (AKJV)

Deuteronomy 26:14-15 I have not eaten thereof in my mourning, neither have I taken away ought thereof for any unclean use, nor given ought thereof for the dead: but I have listened to the voice of the LORD my God, and have done according to all that you have commanded me. Look down from your holy habitation, from heaven, and bless your people Israel, and the land which you have given us, as you swore to our fathers, a land that flows with milk and honey. (AKJV)

Deuteronomy 28:1-2 And it shall come to pass, if you shall listen diligently to the voice of the LORD your God, to observe and to do all his commandments which I command you this day, that the LORD your God will set you on high above all nations of the earth: And all these blessings shall come on you, and overtake you, if you shall listen to the voice of the LORD your God. (AKJV)

Deuteronomy 32:30 How should one chase a thousand, and two put ten thousand to flight, except their Rock had sold them, and the LORD had shut them up? (AKJV)

1 Chronicles 29:14 But who am I, and what is my people, that we should be able to offer so willingly after this sort? for all things come of you, and of your own have we given you. (AKJV)

2 Chronicles 16:9 For the eyes of the LORD run to and fro throughout the whole earth, to show himself strong in the behalf of them whose heart is perfect toward him. (AKJV)

2 Chronicles 30:20 And the LORD listened to Hezekiah, and healed the people. (AKJV)

Psalm 8:4 What is man, that you are mindful of him? and the son of man, that you visit him? (AKJV)

Psalm 20:3-8 Remember all your offerings, and accept your burnt sacrifice; Selah. Grant you according to your own heart, and fulfill all your counsel. We will rejoice in your salvation, and in the name of our God we will set up our banners: the LORD fulfill all your petitions. Now know I that the LORD saves his anointed; he will hear him from his holy heaven with the saving strength of his right hand. Some trust in chariots, and some in horses: but we will remember the name of the LORD our God. They are brought down and fallen: but we are risen, and stand upright. (AKJV)

Psalm 25:14-15 The secret [of the sweet, satisfying companionship] of the Lord have they who fear (revere and worship) Him, and He will show them His covenant and reveal to them its [deep, inner] meaning. My eyes are ever toward the Lord, for He will pluck my feet out of the net (AMP).

Psalm 26:12 My foot stands in an even place; in the congregations I will bless the Lord. (AKJV)

Psalm 41:2-3 The LORD will preserve him, and keep him alive; and he shall be blessed on the earth: and you will not deliver him to the will of his enemies. The LORD will strengthen him on the bed of languishing: you will make all his bed in his sickness. (AKJV)

Psalm 42:11 Why are you cast down, O my soul? and why are you disquieted within me? hope you in God: for I shall yet praise him, who is the health of my countenance, and my God. (AKJV)

Job 33:28 He will deliver his soul from going into the pit, and his life shall see the light. (AKJV)

Job 37:23 Touching the Almighty, we cannot find him out: he is excellent in power, and in judgment, and in plenty of justice: he will not afflict. (AKJV)

Psalm 50:10-12 For every beast of the forest is Mine, {and} the cattle upon a thousand hills {or} upon the mountains where thousands are. I know {and} am acquainted with all the birds of the mountains, and the wild animals of the field are Mine {and} are with Me, in My mind. If I were hungry, I would not tell you, for the world and its fullness are Mine. AMP

Psalm 55:22 Cast your burden on the LORD, and he shall sustain you: he shall never suffer the righteous to be moved. (AKJV)

Psalm 65:4 Blessed is the man whom you choose, and cause to approach to you, that he may dwell in your courts: we shall be satisfied with the goodness of your house, even of your holy temple. (AKJV)

Psalm 72:18-19 Blessed be the LORD God, the God of Israel, who only does wondrous things. And blessed be his glorious name for ever: and let the whole earth be filled with his glory; Amen, and Amen. (AKJV)

Psalm 96:2-4 "...show forth His salvation from day to day. Declare His glory among the nations, His marvelous works among all the peoples. For great is the Lord and greatly to be praised;..." (AKJV)

Psalm 103:12 As far as the east is from the west, so far has He removed our transgressions from us. (AKJV)

Psalm 104:27-28 These wait all on you; that you may give them their meat in due season. That you give them they gather: you open your hand, they are filled with good. (AKJV)

Psalm 112:78 He shall not be afraid of evil tidings; his heart is firmly fixed, trusting (leaning on and being confident) in the Lord. His heart is established and steady, he will not be afraid while he waits to see his desire established upon his adversaries (AMP).

Psalm 118:17 I shall not die, but live, and declare the works of the LORD. (AKJV)

The Blessing Scriptures

Psalm 113:7-8 He raises up the poor out of the dust, and lifts the needy out of the dunghill; That he may set him with princes, even with the princes of his people. (AKJV)

Psalm 145:18-19 The LORD is near to all them that call on him, to all that call on him in truth. He will fulfill the desire of them that fear him: he also will hear their cry, and will save them. (AKJV)

Psalm 147:3 He heals the broken in heart, and binds up their wounds. (AKJV)

Proverbs 3:5-6 Trust in the Lord with all your heart, and lean not on your own understanding; in all your ways acknowledge Him, and He shall direct your paths. (AKJV)

Proverbs 9:11 For by me your days shall be multiplied, and the years of your life shall be increased. (AKJV)

Proverbs 10:5 He who gathers in summer is a wise son, but he who sleeps in harvest is a son who causes shame. AMP

Proverbs 11:23-25 The desire of the righteous is only good: but the expectation of the wicked is wrath. There is that scatters, and yet increases; and there is that withholds more than is meet, but it tends to poverty. The liberal soul shall be made fat: and he that waters shall be watered also himself. (AKJV)

Isaiah 35:1-2 The wilderness and the solitary place shall be glad for them; and the desert shall rejoice, and blossom as the rose. It shall blossom abundantly, and rejoice even with joy and singing: the glory of Lebanon shall be given to it, the excellency of Carmel and Sharon, they shall see the glory of the LORD, and the excellency of

Carmel and Sharon, they shall see the glory of the LORD, and the excellency of our God. (AKJV)

Isaiah 61:1 The Spirit of the Lord GOD is on me; because the LORD has anointed me to preach good tidings to the meek; he has sent me to bind up the broken hearted, to proclaim liberty to the captives, and the opening of the prison to them that are bound; (AKJV)

Isaiah 61:7-8 For your shame you shall have double; and for confusion they shall rejoice in their portion: therefore in their land they shall possess the double: everlasting joy shall be to them. For I the LORD love judgment, I hate robbery for burnt offering; and I will direct their work in truth, and I will make an everlasting covenant with them. (AKJV)

Isaiah 65:22 They shall not build, and another inhabit; they shall not plant, and another eat: for as the days of a tree are the days of my people, and my elect shall long enjoy the work of their hands. (AKJV)

Jeremiah 1:5 Before I formed you in the belly I knew you; and before you came forth out of the womb I sanctified you, and I ordained you a prophet to the nations. (AKJV)

Jeremiah 1:12 Then said the LORD to me, You have well seen: for I will hasten my word to perform it. (AKJV)

Jeremiah 32:27 Behold, I am the LORD, the God of all flesh: is there any thing too hard for me? (AKJV)

Jeremiah 17:7-10 Blessed is the man that trusts in the LORD, and whose hope the LORD is. For he shall be as a tree planted by the waters, and that spreads out her roots by the river, and shall not see when heat comes, but her leaf shall be green; and shall not be careful in the year of drought, neither shall cease from yielding fruit. heart is deceitful above all things, and desperately wicked: who can know it? I the LORD search the heart, I try the reins, even to give every man according to his ways, and according to the fruit of his doings. (AKJV)

Jeremiah 30:16-17 Therefore all they that devour you shall be devoured; and all your adversaries, every one of them, shall go into captivity; and they that spoil you shall be a spoil, and all that prey on you will I give for a prey. For I will restore health to you, and I will heal you of your wounds, said the LORD; because they called you an Outcast, saying, This is Zion, whom no man seeks after. (AKJV)

Jeremiah 33:3 Call unto me, and I will answer thee, and show thee great and mighty things, which thou knowest not. (AKJV)

Jeremiah 42:11-12 Be not afraid of the king of Babylon, of whom you are afraid; be not afraid of him, said the LORD: for I am with you to save you, and to deliver you from his hand. And I will show mercies to you, that he may have mercy on you, and cause you to return to your own land. (AKJV)

Hosea 6:1 Come, and let us return to the LORD: for he has torn, and he will heal us; he has smitten, and he will bind us up. (AKJV)

www.itsmyfootprint.com

Hosea 14:4 I will heal their backsliding, I will love them freely: for my anger is turned away from him. (AKJV)

Malachi 3:6 For I am the LORD, I change not; therefore you sons of Jacob are not consumed. (AKJV)

Matthew 11:28-30 Come to Me, all you who labor and are heavy-laden {and} overburdened, and I will cause you to rest. [I will ease and relieve and refresh your souls.]Take My yoke upon you and learn of Me, for I am gentle (meek) and humble (lowly)   in heart, and you will find rest (relief and ease and refreshment and recreation and blessed quiet) for your souls. For My yoke is wholesome (useful, good--not harsh, hard, sharp, or pressing, but comfortable, gracious, and pleasant), and My burden is light {and} easy to be borne. (AMP)

Matthew 13:44-46 The kingdom of heaven is like something precious buried in a field, which a man found and hid again; then in his joy he goes and sells all he has and buys that field. Again the kingdom of heaven is like a man who is a dealer in search of   fine {and} precious pearls, Who, on finding a single pearl of great price, went and sold all he had and bought it. (AMP)

Matthew 22:37-40 And He replied to him, You shall love the Lord your God with all your heart and with all your soul and with all your mind (intellect). This is the great (most important, principal) and first commandment. And a second is like it: You shall love your neighbor as [you do] yourself. These two commandments sum up {and} upon them depend all the Law and the Prophets. (AMP)

John 10:10 The thief comes only in order to steal and kill and destroy. I came that they may have {and} enjoy life, and have it in abundance (to the full, till it overflows). (AMP)

John 10:27-28 My sheep hear My voice, and I know them, and they follow Me. And I give them eternal life, and they shall never perish; neither shall anyone snatch them out of My hand (NKJV).

Romans 8:2 For the law of the Spirit of life [which is] in Christ Jesus [the law of our new being] has freed me from the law of sin and of death. (AMP)

Romans 8:11 And if the Spirit of Him Who raised up Jesus from the dead dwells in you, [then] He Who raised up Christ {Jesus} from the dead will also restore to life your mortal (short-lived, perishable) bodies through His Spirit Who dwells in you. (AMP)

Romans 8:28-30 We are assured {and} know that [God being a partner in their labor] all things work together {and} are [fitting into a plan] for good to {and} for those who love God and are called according to [His] design {and} purpose. For those whom He foreknew [of whom He was aware and loved beforehand], He also destined from the beginning [foreordaining them] to be molded into the image of His Son [and share inwardly His likeness], that He might become the firstborn among many brethren. And those whom He thus foreordained, He also called; and those whom He called, He also justified (acquitted, made righteous, putting them into right standing with Himself). And those whom He justified, He also glorified [raising them to a heavenly dignity and condition or state of being]. (AMP)

www.itsmyfootprint.com

Galatians 3:13-14 Christ purchased our freedom [redeeming us] from the curse (doom) of the Law [and its condemnation] by [Himself] becoming a curse for us, for it is written [in the Scriptures], Cursed is everyone who hangs on a tree (is crucified); To the end that through [their receiving] Christ Jesus, the blessing [promised] to Abraham might come upon the Gentiles, so that we through faith might [all] receive [the realization of] the promise of the [Holy] Spirit. (AMP)

Galatians 3:26-29 For in Christ Jesus you are all sons of God through faith. For as many [of you] as were baptized into Christ [into a spiritual union and communion with Christ, the Anointed One, the Messiah] have put on (clothed yourselves with) Christ. There is [now no distinction] neither Jew nor Greek, there is neither slave nor free, there is not male and female; for you are all one in Christ Jesus. And if you belong to Christ [are in Him Who is Abraham's Seed], then you are Abraham's offspring and [spiritual] heirs according to promise. (AMP)

Ephesians 2:10 For we are God's [own] handiwork (His workmanship), recreated in Christ Jesus, [born anew] that we may do those good works which God predestined (planned beforehand) for us [taking paths which He prepared ahead of time], that we should walk in them [living the good life which He prearranged and made ready for us to live]. (AMP)

Philippians 2:13 [Not in your own strength] for it is God Who is all the while effectually at work in you [energizing and creating in you the power and desire], both to will and to work for His good pleasure {and} satisfaction {and} delight. (AMP)

Ephesians 2:12 [Remember] that you were at that time separated (living apart) from Christ [excluded from all part in Him], utterly estranged {and} outlawed from the rights of Israel as a nation, and strangers with no share in the sacred compacts of the [Messianic] promise [with no knowledge of or right in God's agreements, His covenants]. And you had no hope (no promise); you were in the world without God. (AMP)

James 1:17 Every good gift and every perfect (free, large, full) gift is from above; it comes down from the Father of all [that gives] light, in [the shining of] Whom there can be no variation [rising or setting] or shadow cast by His turning [as in an eclipse]. (AMP)

1 Peter 2:9 But you are a chosen race, a royal priesthood, a dedicated nation, [God's] own purchased, special people, that you may set forth the wonderful deeds {and} display the virtues and perfections of Him Who called you out of darkness into His marvelous light. (AMP)

1 Peter 2:24 He personally bore our sins in His [own] body on the tree [as on an altar and offered Himself on it], that we might die (cease to exist) to sin and live to righteousness. By His wounds you have been healed. (AMP)

1 John 4:4 Little children, you are of God [you belong to Him] and have [already] defeated {and} overcome them [the agents of the antichrist], because He Who lives in you is greater (mightier) than he who is in the world. (AMP)

Matthew 10:1 AND JESUS summoned to Him His twelve disciples and gave them power {and} authority over unclean spirits, to drive them out, and to cure all kinds of disease and all kinds of weakness {and} infirmity. (AMP)

Mark 10:27 Jesus glanced around at them and said, With men [it is] impossible, but not with God; for all things are possible with God. (AMP)

John 14:12-14 I assure you, most solemnly I tell you, if anyone steadfastly believes in Me, he will himself be able to do the things that I do; and he will do even greater things than these, because I go to the Father. And I will do [I Myself will grant] whatever you ask in My Name [as presenting all that I AM], so that the Father may be glorified {and} extolled in (through) the Son. [Yes] I will grant   [I Myself will do for you] whatever you shall ask in My Name [as presenting all that I AM]. (AMP)

Mark 16:15-18 And He said to them, Go into all the world and preach {and} publish openly the good news (the Gospel) to every creature [of the whole human race]. He who believes [who adheres to and trusts in and relies on the Gospel and Him Whom it sets forth] and is baptized will be saved [from the penalty of eternal death]; but he who does not believe [who does not adhere to and trust in and rely on the Gospel and Him Whom it sets forth] will be condemned. And these attesting signs will accompany those who believe: in My name they will drive out demons; they will speak in new languages; They will pick up serpents; and [even] if they drink anything deadly, it will not hurt them; they will lay their hands on the sick, and they will get well. (AMP)

Luke 1:37 For with God nothing is ever impossible {and} no word from God shall be without power {or} impossible of fulfillment. (AMP)

Acts 10:38 How God anointed {and} consecrated Jesus of Nazareth with the [Holy] Spirit and with strength {and} ability {and} power; how He went about doing good and, in particular, curing all who were harassed {and} oppressed by [the power of] the devil, for God was with Him. (AMP)

Nahum 1:7 The Lord is good, a Strength {and} Stronghold in the day of trouble; He knows (recognizes, has knowledge of, and understands) those who take refuge {and} trust in Him. (AMP)

1 Corinthians 1:9 God is faithful (reliable, trustworthy, and therefore ever true to His promise, and He can be depended on); by Him you were called into companionship {and} participation with His Son, Jesus Christ our Lord. (AMP)

11
Goodness

Psalm 35:27 Let them shout for joy, and be glad, that favor my righteous cause: yes, let them say continually, Let the LORD be magnified, which has pleasure in the prosperity of his servant. (AKJV)

Psalm 31:19 Oh how great is your goodness, which you have laid up for them that fear you; which you have worked for them that trust in you before the sons of men! (AKJV)

Psalm 34:8 O taste and see that the Lord is good: blessed is the man that trusteth in him. (AKJV)

Psalm 34:10 The young lions do lack, and suffer hunger: but they that seek the LORD shall not want any good thing. (AKJV)

Psalm 37:23 The steps of a good man are ordered by the Lord, and He delights in his way. (AKJV)

Psalm 37:3-5 Trust in the LORD, and do good; so shall you dwell in the land, and truly you shall be fed. Delight yourself also in the LORD: and he shall give you the desires of your heart. Commit your way to the LORD; trust also in him; and he shall bring it to pass. (AKJV)

3 John 1:11 Beloved, do not imitate evil, but imitate good. He who does good is of God; he who does evil has not seen (discerned or experienced) God [has enjoyed no vision of Him and does not know Him at all]. (AMP)

Ephesians 2:10 For we are God's [own] handiwork (His workmanship), recreated in Christ Jesus, [born anew] that we may do those good works which God predestined (planned beforehand) for us [taking paths which He prepared ahead of time], that we should walk in them [living the good life which He prearranged and made ready for us to live]. (AMP)

Luke 6:27-28 But I say to you who are listening now to Me: [in order to heed, make it a practice to] love your enemies, treat well (do good to, act nobly toward) those who detest you {and} pursue you with hatred, Invoke blessings upon {and} pray for the happiness of those who curse you, implore God's blessing (favor) upon those who abuse you [who revile, reproach, disparage, and high-handedly misuse you]. (AMP)

Psalm 107:9 For he satisfies the longing soul, and fills the hungry soul with goodness. (AKJV)

12
Grace & Mercy

Hebrews 4:16 Let us then fearlessly and confidently and boldly draw near to the throne of grace (the throne of God's unmerited favor to us sinners), that we may receive mercy [for our failures] and find grace to help in good time for every need [appropriate help and well timed help, coming just when we need it]. (AMP)

Matthew 23:23 Woe to you, scribes and Pharisees, pretenders (hypocrites)! For you give a tenth of your mint and dill and cummin, and have neglected {and} omitted the weightier (more important) matters of the Law--right {and} justice and mercy and fidelity. These you ought [particularly] to have done, without neglecting the others. (AMP)

Ephesians 2:-9 For it is by free grace (God's unmerited favor) that you are saved (delivered from judgment {and} made partakers of Christ's salvation) through [your] faith. And this [salvation] is not of yourselves [of your own doing, it came not through your own striving], but it is the gift of God; Not because of works [not the fulfillment of the Law's demands], lest any man should boast. [It is not the result of what anyone can possibly do, so no one can pride himself in it or take glory to himself.] (AMP)

Ephesians 1:2-3 May grace (God's unmerited favor) and spiritual peace [which means peace with God and harmony, unity, and undisturbedness] be yours from God our Father and from the Lord Jesus Christ. May blessing (praise, laudation, and eulogy) be to the God and Father of our Lord Jesus Christ (the Messiah) Who has blessed us {in Christ} with every spiritual (given by the Holy Spirit) blessing in the heavenly realm! (AMP)

Psalm 84:11-12 For the LORD God is a sun and shield: the LORD will give grace and glory: no good thing will he withhold from them that walk uprightly. O LORD of hosts, blessed is the man that trusts in you. (AKJV)

Ephesians 1:5-8 For He foreordained us (destined us, planned in love for us) to be adopted (revealed) as His own children through Jesus Christ, in accordance with the purpose of His will [because it pleased Him and was His kind intent]-- [So that we might be]   to the praise {and} the commendation of His glorious grace (favor and mercy), which He so freely bestowed on us in the Beloved. In Him we have redemption (deliverance and salvation) through His blood, the remission (forgiveness) of our offenses (shortcomings and trespasses), in accordance with the riches {and} the generosity of His gracious favor, Which He lavished upon us in every kind of wisdom and understanding (practical insight and prudence), (AMP)

Ephesians 2:5 Even when we were dead (slain) by [our own] shortcomings and trespasses, He made us alive together in fellowship and in union with Christ; [He gave us the very life of Christ Himself, the same new life with which He quickened Him, for] it is by grace (His favor and mercy which you did not deserve) that you are saved (delivered from judgment and made partakers of Christ's salvation). (AMP)

Ephesians 2:1-5 AND YOU [He made alive], when you were dead (slain) by [your] trespasses and sins. In which at one time you walked [habitually]. You were following the course {and} fashion of this world [were under the sway of the tendency of this present age], following the prince of the power of the air. [You were obedient to and under the control of] the [demon] spirit that still constantly works in the sons of disobedience [the careless, the rebellious, and the unbelieving, who go against the purposes of God].

Among these we as well as you once lived {and} conducted ourselves in the passions of our flesh [our behavior governed by our corrupt and sensual nature], obeying the impulses of the flesh and the thoughts of the mind [our cravings dictated by our senses and our dark imaginings]. We were then by nature children of [God's] wrath {and} heirs of [His] indignation, like the rest of mankind. But God--so rich is He in His mercy! Because of {and} in order to satisfy the great {and} wonderful {and} intense love with which He loved us,

Even when we were dead (slain) by [our own] shortcomings and trespasses, He made us alive together in fellowship and in union with Christ; [He gave us the very life of Christ Himself, the same new life with which He quickened Him, for] it is by grace (His favor and mercy which you did not deserve) that you are saved (delivered from judgment and made partakers of Christ's salvation). (AMP)

Ephesians 2:6-7 And He raised us up together with Him and made us sit down together [giving us joint seating with Him] in the heavenly sphere [by virtue of our being] in Christ Jesus (the Messiah, the Anointed One). He did this that He might clearly demonstrate through the ages to come the immeasurable (limitless, surpassing) riches of His free grace (His unmerited favor) in [His] kindness {and} goodness of heart toward us in Christ Jesus. (AMP)

Exodus 34:6-7 And the LORD passed by before him, and proclaimed, The LORD, The LORD God, merciful and gracious, long-suffering, and abundant in goodness and truth, Keeping mercy for thousands, forgiving iniquity and transgression and sin, and that will by no means clear the guilty; visiting the iniquity of the fathers on the children, and on the children's children, to the third and to the fourth generation. (AKJV)

64

Psalm 103:17-18 But the mercy of the LORD is from everlasting to everlasting on them that fear him, and his righteousness to children's children; To such as keep his covenant, and to those that remember his commandments to do them. (AKJV)

Psalm 138:8 The Lord will perfect that which concerns me; Your mercy, O Lord, endures forever; do not forsake the works of Your hands. (AKJV)

Lamentations 3:22-23 It is of the LORD's mercies that we are not consumed, because his compassions fail not. They are new every morning: great is your faithfulness. (AKJV)

13
Guidance

John 17: 20-21 My prayer is not for them alone. I also pray for those who will believe in me through their message, that all of them be one, Father, just as you are in me and I am in you. May they also be in us so that the world may believe that you have sent me (NIV)

2 Kings 6:16-17 And he answered, Fear not: for they that be with us are more than they that be with them. And Elisha prayed, and said, LORD, I pray you, open his eyes, that he may see. And the LORD opened the eyes of the young man; and he saw: and, behold, the mountain was full of horses and chariots of fire round about Elisha. (AKJV)

Isaiah 40:31 But they that wait on the LORD shall renew their strength; they shall mount up with wings as eagles; they shall run, and not be weary; and they shall walk, and not faint. (AKJV)

Isaiah 41:10 Fear you not; for I am with you: be not dismayed; for I am your God: I will strengthen you; yes, I will help you; yes, I will uphold you with the right hand of my righteousness. (AKJV)

1 Corinthians 2:16 For who has known {or} understood the mind (the counsels and purposes) of the Lord so as to guide {and} instruct Him {and} give Him knowledge? But we have the mind of Christ (the Messiah) {and} do hold the thoughts (feelings and purposes) of His heart. (AMP)

Psalm 23:1-4 The Lord is my shepherd; I shall not want. He maketh me to lie down in green pastures: he leadeth me beside the still waters. He restoreth my soul: he leadeth me in the paths of righteousness for his name's sake. Yea, though I walk through the valley of the shadow of death, I will fear no evil: for thou art with me; thy rod and thy staff they comfort me. (AKJV)

Isaiah 58:10-11 And if you draw out your soul to the hungry, and satisfy the afflicted soul; then shall your light rise in obscurity, and your darkness be as the noon day: And the LORD shall guide you continually, and satisfy your soul in drought, and make fat your bones: and you shall be like a watered garden, and like a spring of water, whose waters fail not. (AKJV)

14

Honor &

Honesty

3 John 1:4 I have no greater joy than this, to hear that my [spiritual] children are living their lives in the Truth. (AMP)

Exodus 20:12 Honor your father and your mother: that your days may be long on the land which the LORD your God gives you. (AKJV)

Ephesians 4:25-29 Therefore, rejecting all falsity {and} being done now with it, let everyone express the truth with his neighbor, for we are all parts of one body {and} members one of another. When angry, do not sin; do not ever let your wrath (your exasperation, your fury or indignation) last until the sun goes down. Leave no [such] room {or} foothold for the devil [give no opportunity to him]. Let the thief steal no more, but rather let him be industrious, making an honest living with his own hands, so that he may be able to give to those in need. Let no foul {or} polluting language, {nor} evil word {nor} unwholesome {or} worthless talk [ever] come out of your mouth, but only such [speech] as is good {and} beneficial to the spiritual progress of others, as is fitting to the need {and} the occasion, that it may be a blessing {and} give grace (God's favor) to those who hear it. (AMP)

Proverbs 3:9-10 Honor the LORD with your substance, and with the first fruits of all your increase: So shall your barns be filled with plenty, and your presses shall burst out with new wine. (AKJV)

Philippians 4:8 For the rest, brethren, whatever is true, whatever is worthy of reverence {and} is honorable {and} seemly, whatever is just, whatever is pure, whatever is lovely {and} lovable, whatever is kind {and} winsome {and} gracious, if there is any virtue {and} excellence, if there is anything worthy of praise, think on {and} weigh {and} take account of these things [fix your minds on them]. (AMP)

15
Humility

1 Peter 5:5-7 Likewise, you who are younger {and} of lesser rank, be subject to the elders (the ministers and spiritual guides of the church)--[giving them due respect and yielding to their counsel]. Clothe (apron) yourselves, all of you, with humility [as the garb of a servant, so that its covering cannot possibly be stripped from you, with freedom from pride and arrogance] toward one another. For God sets Himself against the proud (the insolent, the overbearing, the disdainful, the presumptuous, the boastful)--[and He opposes, frustrates, and defeats them], but gives grace (favor, blessing) to the humble. Therefore humble yourselves [demote, lower yourselves in your own estimation] under the mighty hand of God, that in due time He may exalt you, Casting the whole of your care [all your anxieties, all your worries, all your concerns, once and for all] on Him, for He cares for you affectionately {and} cares about you watchfully. (AMP)

Matthew 23:12 Whoever exalts himself [with haughtiness and empty pride] shall be humbled (brought low), and whoever humbles himself [whoever has a modest opinion of himself and behaves accordingly] shall be raised to honor. (AMP)

2 Chronicles 31:20-21 And thus did Hezekiah throughout all Judah, and worked that which was good and right and truth before the LORD his God. And in every work that he began in the service of the house of God, and in the law, and in the commandments, to seek his God, he did it with all his heart, and prospered. (AKJV)

Ephesians 5:13 Be subject to one another out of reverence for Christ (the Messiah, the Anointed One). (AMP)

Ephesians 4:1-3 I THEREFORE, the prisoner for the Lord, appeal to {and} beg you to walk (lead a life) worthy of the [divine] calling to which you have been called [with behavior that is a credit to the summons to God's service, Living as becomes you] with complete lowliness of mind (humility) and meekness (unselfishness, gentleness, mildness), with patience, bearing with one another {and} making allowances because you love one another. Be eager {and} strive earnestly to guard {and} keep the harmony {and} oneness of [and produced by] the Spirit in the binding power of peace. (AMP)

Deuteronomy 8:16-18 Who fed you in the wilderness with manna, which your fathers knew not, that he might humble you, and that he might prove you, to do you good at your latter end; And you say in your heart, My power and the might of my hand has gotten me this wealth. But you shall remember the LORD your God: for it is he that gives you power to get wealth, that he may establish his covenant which he swore to your fathers, as it is this day. (AKJV)

Deuteronomy 8:3 He humbled you, causing you to hunger and then feeding you with manna, which neither you nor your ancestors had known, to teach you that man does not live on bread alone but on every word that comes from the mouth of the LORD. (NIV)

1 Peter 3:8-9 Finally, all [of you] should be of one {and} the same mind (united in spirit), sympathizing [with one another], loving [each other] as brethren [of one household], compassionate {and} courteous (tenderhearted and humble). Never return evil for evil or insult for insult (scolding, tongue-lashing, berating), but on the contrary blessing [praying for their welfare, happiness, and protection, and truly pitying and loving them]. For {know that} to this you have been called, that you may yourselves inherit a blessing [from God--that you may obtain a blessing as heirs, bringing welfare and happiness and protection]. (AMP)

16
Integrity

www.itsmyfootprint.com

Mark 4:21-22 And He said to them, Is the lamp brought in to be put under a peck measure or under a bed, and not [to be put] on the lampstand? [Things are hidden temporarily only as a means to revelation.] For there is nothing hidden except to be revealed, nor is anything [temporarily] kept secret except in order that it may be made known. (AMP)

1 John 5:18 We know [absolutely] that anyone born of God does not [deliberately and knowingly] practice committing sin, but the One Who was begotten of God carefully watches over {and} protects him [Christ's divine presence within him preserves him against the evil], and the wicked one does not lay hold (get a grip) on him {or} touch [him]. (AMP)

Ephesians 5:3-4 But immorality (sexual vice) and all impurity [of lustful, rich, wasteful living] or greediness must not even be named among you, as is fitting {and} proper among saints (God's consecrated people). Let there be no filthiness (obscenity, indecency) nor foolish {and} sinful (silly and corrupt) talk, nor coarse jesting, which are not fitting {or} becoming; but instead voice your thankfulness [to God]. (AMP)

Ephesians 5:5-7 For be sure of this: that no person practicing sexual vice or impurity in thought or in life, or one who is covetous [who has lustful desire for the property of others and is greedy for gain]-- for he [in effect] is an idolater--has any inheritance in the kingdom of Christ and of God. Let no one delude {and} deceive you with empty excuses {and} groundless arguments [for these sins], for through these things the wrath of God comes upon the sons of rebellion {and} disobedience. So do not associate {or} be sharers with them. (AMP)

17
Joy & Happiness

www.itsmyfootprint.com

Philippians 4:4 Rejoice in the Lord always: and again I say, Rejoice. (AMP)

1 Thessalonians 5:16-18 Be happy [in your faith] {and} rejoice {and} be glad-hearted continually (always); Be unceasing in prayer [praying perseveringly]; Thank [God] in everything [no matter what the circumstances may be, be thankful and give thanks], for this is the will of God for you [who are] in Christ Jesus [the Revealer and Mediator of that will]. (AMP)

Colossians 3:17 And whatever you do [no matter what it is] in word or deed, do everything in the name of the Lord Jesus {and} in [dependence upon] His Person, giving praise to God the Father through Him. (AMP)

James 1:2-4 Consider it wholly joyful, my brethren, whenever you are enveloped in {or} encounter trials of any sort {or} fall into various temptations. Be assured {and} understand that the   trial {and} proving of your faith bring out endurance {and} steadfastness {and} patience. But let endurance {and} steadfastness {and} patience have full play {and} do a thorough work, so that you may be [people] perfectly and fully developed [with no defects], lacking in nothing. (AMP)

Nehemiah 8:10 Then he said to them, Go your way, eat the fat, and drink the sweet, and send portions to them for whom nothing is prepared: for this day is holy to our LORD: neither be you sorry; for the joy of the LORD is your strength. (AKJV)

Jeremiah 33:9 And it shall be to me a name of joy, a praise and an honor before all the nations of the earth, which shall hear all the good that I do to them: and they shall fear and tremble for all the goodness and for all the prosperity that I procure to it. (AKJV)

2 Corinthians 9:7 Let each one [give] as he has made up his own mind and purposed in his heart, not reluctantly or sorrowfully or under compulsion, for God loves (He takes pleasure in, prizes above other things, and is unwilling to abandon or to do without) a cheerful (joyous, "prompt to do it") giver [whose heart is in his giving]. (AMP)

18
Lifestyle

Romans 12:17-21 Repay no one evil for evil, but take thought for what is honest {and} proper {and} noble [aiming to be above reproach] in the sight of everyone. If possible, as far as it depends on you, live at peace with everyone. Beloved, never avenge yourselves, but leave the way open for [God's] wrath; for it is written, Vengeance is Mine, I will repay (requite), says the Lord. But if your enemy is hungry, feed him; if he is thirsty, give him drink; for by so doing you will heap burning coals upon his head. Do not let yourself be overcome by evil, but overcome (master) evil with good. (AMP)

Ephesians 4:17 So this I say and solemnly testify in [the name of] the Lord [as in His presence], that you must no longer live as the heathen (the Gentiles) do in their perverseness [in the folly, vanity, and emptiness of their souls and the futility] of their minds. (AMP)

Ephesians 4:22 Strip yourselves of your former nature [put off and discard your old unrenewed-self] which characterized your previous manner of life and becomes corrupt through lusts {and} desires that spring from delusion; (AMP)

Ephesians 5:15-17 Look carefully then how you walk! Live purposefully {and} worthily {and} accurately, not as the unwise {and} witless, but as wise (sensible, intelligent people), Making the very most of the time [buying up each opportunity], because the days are evil. Therefore do not be vague {and} thoughtless {and} foolish, but understanding {and} firmly grasping what the will of the Lord is. (AMP)

Hebrews 13:5 Let your character {or} moral disposition be free from love of money [including greed, avarice, lust, and craving for earthly possessions] and be satisfied with your present [circumstances and with what you have]; for He [God] Himself has said, I will not in any way fail you {nor} give you up {nor} leave you without support. [I will] not, [I will] not, [I will] not in any degree leave you helpless {nor} forsake {nor} let [you] down (relax My hold on you)! [Assuredly not!] (AMP)

1 John 1:7 But if we [really] are living and walking in the Light, as He [Himself] is in the Light, we have [true, unbroken] fellowship with one another, and the blood of Jesus Christ His Son cleanses (removes) us from all sin and guilt [keeps us cleansed from sin in all its forms and manifestations]. (AMP)

1 Corinthians 1:27 [No] for God selected (deliberately chose) what in the world is foolish to put the wise to shame, and what the world calls weak to put the strong to shame. (AMP)

James 4:7 So be subject to God. Resist the devil [stand firm against him], and he will flee from you (AMP).

1 Peter 5:8 Be well balanced (temperate, sober of mind), be vigilant and cautious at all times; for that enemy of yours, the devil, roams around like a lion roaring [in fierce hunger], seeking someone to seize upon and devour. (AMP)

www.itsmyfootprint.com

Galatians 5:22 But the fruit of the [Holy] Spirit [the work which His presence within accomplishes] is love, joy (gladness), peace, patience (an even temper, forbearance), kindness, goodness (benevolence), faithfulness, Gentleness (meekness, humility), self-control (self-restraint, continence). Against such things there is no law [that can bring a charge]. And those who belong to Christ Jesus (the Messiah) have crucified the flesh (the godless human nature) with its passions and appetites {and} desires. (AMP)

Ephesians 6:10 In conclusion, be strong in the Lord [be empowered through your union with Him]; draw your strength from Him [that strength which His boundless might provides]. Put on God's whole armor [the armor of a heavy-armed soldier which God supplies], that you may be able successfully to stand up against [all] the strategies {and} the deceits of the devil. (AMP)

19
Love

1 Timothy 1:5 Whereas the object {and} purpose of our instruction {and} charge is love, which springs from a pure heart and a good (clear) conscience and sincere (unfeigned) faith. (AMP)

John 13:34-35 A new commandment I give you that you love one another. As I have loved you, so you must love one another. By this all men will know that you are my disciples , if you love one another. (NIV)

Romans 12:9-12 [Let your] love be sincere (a real thing); hate what is evil [loathe all ungodliness, turn in horror from wickedness], but hold fast to that which is good. Love one another with brotherly affection [as members of one family], giving precedence {and} showing honor to one another. Never lag in zeal {and} in earnest endeavor; be aglow {and} burning with the Spirit, serving the Lord. Rejoice {and} exult in hope; be steadfast and patient in   suffering {and} tribulation; be constant in prayer. (AMP)

1 Peter 3:8-9 Finally, all [of you] should be of one {and} the same mind (united in spirit), sympathizing [with one another], loving [each other] as brethren [of one household], compassionate {and} courteous (tender-hearted and humble). Never return evil for evil or insult for insult (scolding, tongue-lashing, berating), but on the contrary blessing [praying for their welfare, happiness, and protection, and truly pitying and loving them]. For {know that} to this you have been called, that you may yourselves inherit a blessing [from God--that you may obtain a blessing as heirs, bringing welfare and happiness and protection]. (AMP)

1 John 4:17-18 Love has been perfected among us in this: that we may have boldness in the day of judgment; because as He is, so are we in this world. There is no fear in love; but perfect love casts out fear, because fear involves torment. But he who fears has not been made perfect in love (NKJV).

Romans 8:31-35 What then shall we say to [all] this? If God is for us, who [can be] against us? [Who can be our foe, if God is on our side?] He who did not withhold {or} spare [even] His own Son but gave Him up for us all, will He not also with Him freely {and} graciously give us all [other] things? Who shall bring any charge against God's elect [when it is] God Who justifies [that is, Who puts us in right relation to Himself? Who shall come forward and accuse or impeach those whom God has chosen? Will God, Who acquits us?] Who is there to condemn [us]? Will Christ Jesus (the Messiah), Who died, or rather Who was raised from the dead, Who is at the right hand of God actually pleading {as} He intercedes for us? Who shall ever separate us from Christ's love? Shall suffering {and} affliction {and} tribulation? Or calamity {and} distress? Or persecution or hunger or destitution or peril or sword? (AMP)

1 Corinthians 13:4-7 Love endures long {and} is patient and kind; love never is envious {nor} boils over with jealousy, is not boastful {or} vainglorious, does not display itself haughtily. It is not conceited (arrogant and inflated with pride); it is not rude (unmannerly) {and} does not act unbecomingly. Love (God's love in us) does not insist on its own rights {or} its own way, {for} it is not self-seeking; it is not touchy {or} fretful {or} resentful; it takes no account of the evil done to it [it pays no attention to a suffered wrong]. It does not rejoice at injustice {and} unrighteousness, but rejoices when right {and} truth prevail. Love bears up under anything {and} everything that comes, is ever ready to believe the best of every person, its hopes are fadeless under all circumstances, and it endures everything [without weakening]. (AMP)

86

2 Timothy 1:7 For God has not given us a spirit of fear, but of power and of love and of a sound mind (NKJV).

Romans 8:35-37 Who shall ever separate us from Christ's love? Shall suffering {and} affliction {and} tribulation? Or calamity {and} distress? Or persecution or hunger or destitution or peril or sword? Even as it is written, For Thy sake we are put to death all the day long; we are regarded {and} counted as sheep for the slaughter. Yet amid all these things we are more than conquerors {and} gain a surpassing victory through Him Who loved us. (AMP)

Romans 12:9-13 [Let your] love be sincere (a real thing); hate what is evil [loathe all ungodliness, turn in horror from wickedness], but hold fast to that which is good. Love one another with brotherly affection [as members of one family], giving precedence {and} showing honor to one another. Never lag in zeal {and} in earnest endeavor; be aglow {and} burning with the Spirit, serving the Lord. Rejoice {and} exult in hope; be steadfast and patient in   suffering {and} tribulation; be constant in prayer. Contribute to the needs of God's people [sharing in the necessities of the saints]; pursue the practice of hospitality. (AMP)

1 Peter 4:7-8 But the end {and} culmination of all things has now come near; keep sound minded {and} self-restrained and alert therefore for [the practice of] prayer. Above all things have intense {and} unfailing love for one another, for love covers a multitude of sins [forgives and disregards the offenses of others]. (AMP)

20
Obedience

Proverbs 13:18 Poverty and shame shall be to him that refuses instruction: but he that regards reproof shall be honored. (AKJV)

Ephesians 6:5-8 Servants (slaves), be obedient to those who are your physical masters, having respect for them and eager concern to please them, in singleness of motive {and} with all your heart, as [service] to Christ [Himself]-- Not in the way of eye-service [as if they were watching you] and only to please men, but as servants (slaves) of Christ, doing the will of God heartily {and} with your whole soul; Rendering service readily with goodwill, as to the Lord and not to men, Knowing that for whatever good anyone does, he will receive his reward from the Lord, whether he is slave or free. (AMP)

Philippians 2:14-15 Do all things without grumbling {and} faultfinding {and} complaining [against God] and questioning {and} doubting [among yourselves], That you may show yourselves to be blameless {and} guileless, innocent {and} uncontaminated, children of God without blemish (faultless, unrebukable) in the midst of a crooked {and} wicked generation [spiritually perverted and perverse], among whom you are seen as bright lights (stars or beacons shining out clearly) in the [dark] world, (AMP)

Isaiah 1:19 If you be willing and obedient, you shall eat the good of the land: (AKJV)

James 1:22-25 But be doers of the Word [obey the message], and not merely listeners to it, betraying yourselves [into deception by reasoning contrary to the Truth]. For if anyone only listens to the Word without obeying it {and} being a doer of it, he is like a man who looks carefully at his [own] natural face in a mirror; For he thoughtfully observes himself, and then goes off and promptly forgets what he was like. But he who looks carefully into the faultless law, the [law] of liberty, and is faithful to it {and} perseveres in looking into it, being not a heedless listener who forgets but an active doer [who obeys], he shall be blessed in his doing (his life of obedience). (AMP)

Genesis 22:18 And in your Seed [Christ] shall all the nations of the earth be blessed and [by Him] bless themselves, because you have heard and obeyed My voice (AMP).

Job 36:11 If they obey and serve him, they shall spend their days in prosperity, and their years in pleasures. (AKJV)

James 2:17 So also faith, if it does not have works (deeds and actions of obedience to back it up), by itself is destitute of power (inoperative, dead). (AMP).

21
Peace & Security

Colossians 3:15 And let the peace (soul harmony which comes) from Christ rule (act as umpire continually) in your hearts [deciding and settling with finality all questions that arise in your minds, in that peaceful state] to which as [members of Christ's] one body you were also called [to live]. And be thankful (appreciative), [giving praise to God always]. (AMP)

Hebrews 12:14 Strive to live in peace with everybody and pursue that consecration {and} holiness without which no one will [ever] see the Lord. (AMP)

Philippians 4:6 Do not fret {or} have any anxiety about anything, but in every circumstance {and} in everything, by prayer and petition (definite requests), with thanksgiving, continue to make your wants known to God. (AMP)

Psalm 29:11 The LORD will give strength to his people; the LORD will bless his people with peace. (AKJV)

Proverbs 3:1-2 My son, forget not my law; but let your heart keep my commandments: For length of days, and long life, and peace, shall they add to you. (AKJV)

Job 22:21 Acquaint now yourself with him, and be at peace: thereby good shall come to you. (AKJV)

Deuteronomy 31:6 Be strong and of a good courage, fear not, nor be afraid of them: for the LORD your God, he it is that does go with you; he will not fail you, nor forsake you. (AKJV)

.

www.itsmyfootprint.com

James 3:14-18 But if you have bitter jealousy (envy) and contention (rivalry, selfish ambition) in your hearts, do not pride yourselves on it and thus be in defiance of {and} false to the Truth. This [superficial] wisdom is not such as comes down from above, but is earthly, unspiritual (animal), even devilish (demoniacal). For wherever there is jealousy (envy) and contention (rivalry and selfish ambition), there will also be confusion (unrest, disharmony, rebellion) and all sorts of evil {and} vile practices. But the wisdom from above is first of all pure (undefiled); then it is peace-loving, courteous (considerate, gentle). [It is willing to] yield to reason, full of compassion and good fruits; it is wholehearted {and} straightforward, impartial {and} unfeigned (free from doubts, wavering, and insincerity). And the harvest of righteousness (of conformity to God's will in thought and deed) is [the fruit of the seed] sown in peace by those who work for {and} make peace [in themselves and in others, that peace which means concord, agreement, and harmony between individuals, with undisturbedness, in a peaceful mind free from fears and agitating passions and moral conflicts]. (AMP)

Deuteronomy 31:8 And the LORD, he it is that does go before you; he will be with you, he will not fail you, neither forsake you: fear not, neither be dismayed. (AKJV)

Matthew 10:29-31 Are not two little sparrows sold for a penny? And yet not one of them will fall to the ground without your Father's leave (consent) {and} notice. But even the very hairs of your head are all numbered. Fear not, then; you are of more value than many sparrows. (AMP)

www.itsmyfootprint.com

22
Righteousness

Psalm 92:12-15 The righteous shall flourish like the palm tree: he shall grow like a cedar in Lebanon. Those that be planted in the house of the LORD shall flourish in the courts of our God. They shall still bring forth fruit in old age; they shall be fat and flourishing; To show that the LORD is upright: he is my rock, and there is no unrighteousness in him. (AKJV)

Romans 12:1 I appeal to you therefore, brethren, and beg of you in view of [all] the mercies of God, to make a decisive dedication of your bodies [presenting all your members and faculties] as a living sacrifice, holy (devoted, consecrated) and well pleasing to God, which is your reasonable (rational, intelligent) service and spiritual worship. (AMP)

Romans 12:1-2 I APPEAL to you therefore, brethren, {and} beg of you in view of [all] the mercies of God, to make a decisive dedication of your bodies [presenting all your members and faculties] as a living sacrifice, holy (devoted, consecrated) and well pleasing to God, which is your reasonable (rational, intelligent) service {and} spiritual worship. Do not be conformed to this world (this age), [fashioned after and adapted to its external, superficial customs], but be transformed (changed) by the [entire] renewal of your mind [by its new ideals and its new attitude], so that you may prove [for yourselves] what is the good and acceptable and perfect will of God, {even} the thing which is good and acceptable and perfect [in His sight for you]. (AMP)

Romans 14:17 [After all] the kingdom of God is not a matter of [getting the] food and drink [one likes], but instead it is righteousness (that state which makes a person acceptable to God) and [heart] peace and joy in the Holy Spirit. (AMP)

Genesis 6:9 These are the generations of Noah: Noah was a just man and perfect in his generations, and Noah walked with God. (AKJV)

Psalm 5:12 For you, LORD, will bless the righteous; with favor will you compass him as with a shield. (AKJV)

Proverbs 24:16 For a righteous man may fall seven times and rise again, but the wicked shall fall by calamity. (AKJV)

Isaiah 3:10 Say you to the righteous, that it shall be well with him: for they shall eat the fruit of their doings. (AKJV)

Matthew 6:33 But seek (aim at and strive after) first of all His kingdom and His righteousness (His way of doing and being right), and then all these things taken together will be given you besides. (AMP)

Psalm 37:25-26 I have been young, and now am old; yet have I not seen the righteous forsaken, nor his seed begging bread. He is ever merciful, and lends; and his seed is blessed. (AKJV)

Proverbs 8:17-21 I love them that love me; and those that seek me early shall find me. Riches and honor are with me; yes, durable riches and righteousness. My fruit is better than gold, yes, than fine gold; and my revenue than choice silver. I lead in the way of righteousness, in the middle of the paths of judgment: That I may cause those that love me to inherit substance; and I will fill their treasures. (AKJV)

2 Corinthians 5:21 For our sake He made Christ [virtually] to be sin Who knew no sin, so that in and through Him we might become [endued with, viewed as being in, and examples of] the righteousness of God [what we ought to be, approved and acceptable and in right relationship with Him, by His goodness]. (AMP)

1 Peter 3:12-13 For the eyes of the Lord are upon the righteous (those who are upright and in right standing with God), and His ears are attentive to their prayer. But the face of the Lord is against those who practice evil [to oppose them, to frustrate, and defeat them]. Now who is there to hurt you if you are zealous followers of that which is good? (AMP)

.

23
Speech

Proverbs 15:4 A wholesome tongue is a tree of life, but perverseness in it breaks the spirit. (AKJV)

Proverbs 16:24 Pleasant words are as an honeycomb, sweet to the soul, and health to the bones. (AKJV)

Proverbs 18:21 Death and life are in the power of the tongue: and they that love it shall eat the fruit thereof. (AKJV**)**

Proverbs 12:13-14, 21 The wicked is snared by the transgression of his lips: but the just shall come out of trouble. A man shall be satisfied with good by the fruit of his mouth: and the recompense of a man's hands shall be rendered unto him. There shall no evil happen to the just: but the wicked shall be filled with mischief. (AKJV)

Proverbs 27:2 Let another man praise thee, and not thine own mouth; a stranger, and not thine own lips. (AKJV)

Proverbs 12:18 There is that speaks like the piercings of a sword: but the tongue of the wise is health. (AKJV)

Ephesians 4:31-32 Let all bitterness and indignation {and} wrath (passion, rage, bad temper) and resentment (anger, animosity) and quarreling (brawling, clamor, contention) and slander (evil-speaking, abusive or blasphemous language) be banished from you, with all malice (spite, ill will, or baseness of any kind). And become useful {and} helpful {and} kind to one another, tenderhearted (compassionate, understanding, loving-hearted), forgiving one another [readily and freely], as God in Christ forgave you. (AMP)

24
Wealth

Proverbs 13:11 Wealth [not earned but] won in haste {or} unjustly {or} from the production of things for vain {or} detrimental use [such riches] will dwindle away, but he who gathers little by little will increase [his riches]. AMP

Proverbs 13:22 A good man leaves an inheritance to his children's children: and the wealth of the sinner is laid up for the just. (AKJV)

Luke 12:15 And He said to them, Guard yourselves and keep free from all covetousness (the immoderate desire for wealth, the greedy longing to have more); for a man's life does not consist in {and} is not derived from possessing overflowing abundance {or} that which is over and above his needs. (AMP)

1 Timothy 6:17-19 As for the rich in this world, charge them not to be proud {and} arrogant {and} contemptuous of others, nor to set their hopes on uncertain riches, but on God, Who richly {and} ceaselessly provides us with everything for [our] enjoyment. [Charge them] to do good, to be rich in good works, to be liberal {and} generous of heart, ready to share [with others], In this way laying up for themselves [the riches that endure forever as] a good foundation for the future, so that they may grasp that which is life indeed. (AMP)

Psalm 37:21-22 The wicked borrows, and pays not again: but the righteous shows mercy, and gives. For such as be blessed of him shall inherit the earth; and they that be cursed of him shall be cut off. (AKJV)

.

Proverbs 22:7-9 The rich rules over the poor, and the borrower is servant to the lender. He that sows iniquity shall reap vanity: and the rod of his anger shall fail. He that has a bountiful eye shall be blessed; for he gives of his bread to the poor. (AKJV)

Proverbs 10:22 The blessing of the LORD, it makes rich, and he adds no sorrow with it. (AKJV)

25
Wisdom

Proverbs 13:20-21 He that walks with wise men shall be wise: but a companion of fools shall be destroyed. Evil pursues sinners: but to the righteous good shall be repaid. (AKJV)

Proverbs 19:20 Hear counsel, receive instruction, {and} accept correction, that you may be wise in the time to come. AMP

Habakkuk 2:2 And the Lord answered me, and said, Write the vision, and make it plain upon tables, that he may run that readeth it. (AKJV)

Colossians 1:9-10 For this reason we also, from the day we heard of it, have not ceased to pray {and} make [special] request for you, [asking] that you may be filled with the full (deep and clear) knowledge of His will in all spiritual wisdom [in comprehensive insight into the ways and purposes of God] and in understanding {and} discernment of spiritual things-- That you may walk (live and conduct yourselves) in a manner worthy of the Lord, fully pleasing to Him {and} desiring to please Him in all things, bearing fruit in every good work and steadily growing {and} increasing in {and} by the knowledge of God [with fuller, deeper, and clearer insight, acquaintance, and recognition]. (AMP)

Colossians 4:5-6 Behave yourselves wisely [living prudently and with discretion] in your relations with those of the outside world (the non-Christians), making the very most of the time {and} seizing (buying up) the opportunity. Let your speech at all times be gracious (pleasant and winsome), seasoned [as it were] with salt, [so that you may never be at a loss] to know how you ought to answer anyone [who puts a question to you]. (AMP)

Proverbs 3:13-16 Happy is the man that finds wisdom, and the man that gets understanding. For the merchandise of it is better than the merchandise of silver, and the gain thereof than fine gold. She is more precious than rubies: and all the things you can desire are not to be compared to her. Length of days is in her right hand; and in her left hand riches and honor. (AKJV)

James 1:5 If any of you lacks wisdom, let him ask of God, who gives to all liberally and without reproach, and it will be given to him (NKJV).

Ephesians 3:9-11 Also to enlighten all men {and} make plain to them what is the plan [regarding the Gentiles and providing for the salvation of all men] of the mystery kept hidden through the ages {and} concealed until now in [the mind of] God Who created all things {by Christ Jesus.} [The purpose is] that through the church the complicated, many-sided wisdom of God in all its infinite variety {and} innumerable aspects might now be made known to the angelic rulers and authorities (principalities and powers) in the heavenly sphere. This is in accordance with the terms of the eternal {and} timeless purpose which He has realized {and} carried into effect in [the person of] Christ Jesus our Lord, (AMP)

James 3:14-16 But if you have bitter jealousy (envy) and contention (rivalry, selfish ambition) in your hearts, do not pride yourselves on it and thus be in defiance of {and} false to the Truth. This [superficial] wisdom is not such as comes down from above, but is earthly, unspiritual (animal), even devilish (demoniacal). For wherever there is jealousy (envy) and contention (rivalry and selfish ambition), there will also be confusion (unrest, disharmony, rebellion) and all sorts of evil {and} vile practices. (AMP)

26
Protection

Psalm 91:7 A thousand may fall at your side, and ten thousand at your right hand, but it shall not come near you (AMP).

Romans 8:38-39 For I am persuaded beyond doubt (am sure) that neither death nor life, nor angels nor principalities, nor things impending {and} threatening nor things to come, nor powers, Nor height nor depth, nor anything else in all creation will be able to separate us from the love of God which is in Christ Jesus our Lord. (AMP)

Romans 8:31-32 What then shall we say to [all] this? If God is for us, who [can be] against us? [Who can be our foe, if God is on our side?] He who did not withhold {or} spare [even] His own Son but gave Him up for us all, will He not also with Him freely {and} graciously give us all [other] things? (AMP)

Deuteronomy 6:18-19 And you shall do that which is right and good in the sight of the LORD: that it may be well with you, and that you may go in and possess the good land which the LORD swore to your fathers. To cast out all your enemies from before you, as the LORD has spoken. (AKJV)

Ephesians 3:18-19 That you may have the power {and} be strong to apprehend {and} grasp with all the saints [God's devoted people, the experience of that love] what is the breadth and length and height and depth [of it]; [That you may really come] to know [practically, through experience for yourselves] the love of Christ, which far surpasses mere knowledge [without experience]; that you may be filled [through all your being] unto all the fullness of God [may have the richest measure of the divine Presence, and become a body wholly filled and flooded with God Himself]! (AMP)

27
The Word of God

Hebrew 4:12 For the word of God is living and active sharper than any two edged sword, it penetrates even to diving soul and spirit, joints and marrow, it judges the thoughts and attitudes of the heart. (NIV)

John 1: 1 In the beginning was the Word and the Word was with God and the Word was God. (NIV)

John 1: 4-5 In him was life, and that life the light men. The light shines in the darkness, but the darkness has not understood it. (NIV)

Jeremiah 23:29 "Is not my word like fire," declares the Lord, "and like a hammer that breaks a rock in pieces? (NIV)

Isaiah 55:10-11 For as the rain comes down, and the snow from heaven, and returns not thither, but waters the earth, and makes it bring forth and bud, that it may give seed to the sower, and bread to the eater: So shall my word be that goes forth out of my mouth: it shall not return to me void, but it shall accomplish that which I please, and it shall prosper in the thing whereto I sent it. (AKJV)

Psalm 107:20 He sent his word, and healed them, and delivered them from their destructions. (AKJV)

Psalm 119: 32 I run in the path of your commands, for you have set my heart free. (NIV)

Psalm 119: 32 Turn my eyes away from worthless things; preserve my life according to your Word. (NIV)

Psalms 19:7-11 The law of the Lord is perfect, reviving the soul. The statutes of the Lord are trustworthy making wise the simple. The precepts of the Lord are right, giving joy to the heart. The commands of the Lord are radiant, giving light to the eyes. The fear of the Lord is pure, enduring forever. The ordinances of the Lord are sure and altogether righteous. They are more precious than gold, than much pure gold, they are sweeter than honey, than honey from the comb. By them is your servant warned, in keeping the there is great reward. (NIV)

Psalm 119: 103 How sweet are your words to my taste, sweeter than honey to my mouth! (NIV)

John 15: 7 If you remain in me and my words remain in you, ask whatever you wish, and it will be done for you. (NIV)

Mathew 24:35 Heaven and earth will pass away, but my words will never pass away. (NIV)

Psalm 119:105 Your word is a lamp to my feet and a light to my path. (AKJV)

Joshua 1:8 Keep this Book of the Law always on your lips; meditate on it day and night, so that you may be careful to do everything written in it. Then you will be prosperous and successful. (NIV)

Deuteronomy 11:18 Fix these words of mine in your hearts and minds; tie them as symbols on your hands and bind them on your foreheads. (NIV)

Deuteronomy 29:9 Keep therefore the words of this covenant, and do them, that you may prosper in all that you do. (AKJV)

www.itsmyfootprint.com

Deuteronomy 26:16-19 This day the LORD your God has commanded you to do these statutes and judgments: you shall therefore keep and do them with all your heart, and with all your soul. You have avouched the LORD this day to be your God, and to walk in his ways, and to keep his statutes, and his commandments, and his judgments, and to listen to his voice: And the LORD has avouched you this day to be his peculiar people, as he has promised you, and that you should keep all his commandments; And to make you high above all nations which he has made, in praise, and in name, and in honor; and that you may be an holy people to the LORD your God, as he has spoken. (AKJV)

Matthew 4:4 But He replied, It has been written, Man shall not live {and} be upheld {and} sustained by bread alone, but by every word that comes forth from the mouth of God. (AMP)

John 8:31-32 So Jesus said to those Jews who had believed in Him, If you abide in My word [hold fast to My teachings and live in accordance with them], you are truly My disciples. And you will know the Truth, and the Truth will set you free. (AMP)

2 Timothy 2:15 Study and be eager and do your utmost to present yourself to God approved (tested by trial), a workman who has no cause to be ashamed, correctly analyzing and accurately dividing [rightly handling and skillfully teaching] the Word of Truth. (AMP)

Psalm 119:9 How can a young person stay on the path of purity? By living according to your word (NIV)

Matthew 25:29-30 ... For to everyone who has will more be given, and he will be furnished richly so that he will have an abundance; but from the one who does not have, even what he does have will be taken away. And throw the good-for-nothing servant into the outer darkness; there will be weeping and grinding of teeth. (AMP)

Hebrews 4:12 For the Word that God speaks is alive and full of power [making it active, operative, energizing, and effective]; it is sharper than any two-edged sword, penetrating to the dividing line of the breath of life (soul) and [the immortal] spirit, and of joints and marrow [of the deepest parts of our nature], exposing {and} sifting {and} analyzing {and} judging the very thoughts and purposes of the heart. (AMP)

1 Peter 1:23-25 You have been regenerated (born again), not from a mortal origin (seed, sperm), but from one that is immortal by the {ever} living and lasting Word of God. For all flesh (mankind) is like grass, and all its glory (honor) like [the] flower of grass. The grass withers and the flower drops off, But the Word of the Lord (divine instruction, the Gospel) endures forever. And this Word is the good news which was preached to you. (AMP)

28
Confession

www.itsmyfootprint.com

Romans 10:9-13 Because if you acknowledge {and} confess with your lips that Jesus is Lord and in your heart believe (adhere to, trust in, and rely on the truth) that God raised Him from the dead, you will be saved. For with the heart a person believes (adheres to, trusts in, and relies on Christ) and so is justified (declared righteous, acceptable to God), and with the mouth he confesses (declares openly and speaks out freely his faith) {and} confirms [his] salvation. The Scripture says, No man who believes in Him [who adheres to, relies on, and trusts in Him] will [ever] be put to shame {or} be disappointed. [No one] for there is no distinction between Jew and Greek. The same Lord is Lord over all [of us] and He generously bestows His riches upon all who call upon Him [in faith]. For everyone who calls upon the name of the Lord [invoking Him as Lord] will be saved. (AMP)

Romans 10:17 So faith comes by hearing [what is told], and what is heard comes by the preaching [of the message that came from the lips] of Christ (the Messiah Himself). (AMP)

Psalms 119: 11 I have hidden your word in my heart that I might not sin against you. (NIV)

Psalm 119: 172 May my tongue sing of your word, for all your commands are righteous. (NIV)

Deuteronomy 11:22-24 For if you shall diligently keep all these commandments which I command you, to do them, to love the LORD your God, to walk in all his ways, and to join to him; Then will the LORD drive out all these nations from before you, and you shall possess greater nations and mightier than yourselves. Every place where on the soles of your feet shall tread shall be yours: (AKJV)

Romans 10:9-13 Because if you acknowledge {and} confess with your lips that Jesus is Lord and in your heart believe (adhere to, trust in, and rely on the truth) that God raised Him from the dead, you will be saved. For with the heart a person believes (adheres to, trusts in, and relies on Christ) and so is justified (declared righteous, acceptable to God), and with the mouth he confesses (declares openly and speaks out freely his faith) {and} confirms [his] salvation. The Scripture says, No man who believes in Him [who adheres to, relies on, and trusts in Him] will [ever] be put to shame {or} be disappointed. [No one] for there is no distinction between Jew and Greek. The same Lord is Lord over all [of us] and He generously bestows His riches upon all who call upon Him [in faith]. For everyone who calls upon the name of the Lord [invoking Him as Lord] will be saved. (AMP)

Romans 10:17 So faith comes by hearing [what is told], and what is heard comes by the preaching [of the message that came from the lips] of Christ (the Messiah Himself). (AMP)

Psalms 119: 11 I have hidden your word in my heart that I might not sin against you. (NIV)

Psalm 119: 172 May my tongue sing of your word, for all your commands are righteous. (NIV)

Deuteronomy 11:22-24 For if you shall diligently keep all these commandments which I command you, to do them, to love the LORD your God, to walk in all his ways, and to join to him; Then will the LORD drive out all these nations from before you, and you shall possess greater nations and mightier than yourselves. Every place where on the soles of your feet shall tread shall be yours: (AKJV)

Deuteronomy 11:18-21 Therefore shall you lay up these my words in your heart and in your soul, and bind them for a sign on your hand, that they may be as frontlets between your eyes. And you shall teach them your children, speaking of them when you sit in your house, and when you walk by the way, when you lie down, and when you rise up. And you shall write them on the door posts of your house, and on your gates: That your days may be multiplied, and the days of your children, in the land which the LORD swore to your fathers to give them, as the days of heaven on the earth. (AKJV)

Deuteronomy 6:6-9 These commandments that I give you today are to be on your hearts. Impress them on your children. Talk about them when you sit at home and when you walk along the road, when you lie down and when you get up. Tie them as symbols on your hands and bind them on your foreheads. Write them on the doorframes of your houses and on your gates. (NIV)

29
Faith & Hope

Ephesians 3:20 Now to Him Who, by (in consequence of) the [action of His] power that is at work within us, is able to [carry out His purpose and] do superabundantly, far over {and} above all that we [dare] ask or think [infinitely beyond our highest prayers, desires, thoughts, hopes, or dreams]-- (AMP**)**

Philippians 1:6 And I am convinced {and} sure of this very thing, that He Who began a good work in you will continue until the day of Jesus Christ [right up to the time of His return], developing [that good work] {and} perfecting {and} bringing it to full completion in you. (AMP)

Philippians 3:13 Brethren, I do not count myself to have apprehended; but one thing I do, forgetting those things which are behind and reaching forward to those things which are ahead (NKJV).

1 Timothy 6:6-9 [And it is, indeed, a source of immense profit, for] godliness accompanied with contentment (that contentment which is a sense of inward sufficiency) is great {and} abundant gain. For we brought nothing into the world, and {obviously} we cannot take anything out of the world; But if we have food and clothing, with these we shall be content (satisfied). But those who crave to be rich fall into temptation and a snare and into many foolish (useless, godless) and hurtful desires that plunge men into ruin {and} destruction and miserable perishing. (AMP)

Hebrews 10:35-36 Do not, therefore, fling away your fearless confidence, for it carries a great {and} glorious compensation of reward. For you have need of steadfast patience {and} endurance, so that you may perform {and} fully accomplish the will of God, and thus receive {and} carry away [and enjoy to the full] what is (AMP)

118

30
Daily Life

Ephesians 6:13 Therefore put on God's complete armor, that you may be able to resist {and} stand your ground on the evil day [of danger], and, having done all [the crisis demands], to stand [firmly in your place]. (AMP)

Philemon 1:6 [And I pray] that the participation in {and} sharing of your faith may produce {and} promote full recognition {and} appreciation {and} understanding {and} precise knowledge of every good [thing] that is ours in [our identification with] Christ {Jesus} [and unto His glory]. (AMP)

Romans 12:14-16 Bless those who persecute you [who are cruel in their attitude toward you]; bless and do not curse them. Rejoice with those who rejoice [sharing others' joy], and weep with those who weep [sharing others' grief]. Live in harmony with one another; do not be haughty (snobbish, high-minded, exclusive), but readily adjust yourself to [people, things] {and} give yourselves to humble tasks. Never overestimate yourself {or} be wise in your own conceits. (AMP)

2 John 1:8 Look to yourselves (take care) that you may not lose (throw away or destroy) all that we {and} you have labored for, but that you may [persevere until you] win {and} receive back a perfect reward [in full]. AMP)

Ephesians 5:10-12 And try to learn [in your experience] what is pleasing to the Lord [let your lives be constant proofs of what is most acceptable to Him]. Take no part in {and} have no fellowship with the fruitless deeds {and} enterprises of darkness, but instead [let your lives be so in contrast as to] expose {and} reprove {and} convict them. For it is a shame even to speak of {or} mention the things that [such people] practice in secret. (AMP)

The Blessing Scriptures

Ephesians 5:8 For once you were darkness, but now you are light in the Lord; walk as children of Light [lead the lives of those native-born to the Light]. (AMP)

www.itsmyfootprint.com

31
Victory

Proverbs 21:31 The horse is prepared against the day of battle: but safety is of the LORD. (AKJV)

1 John 5:4 For whatever is born of God is victorious over the world; and this is the victory that conquers the world, even our faith. (AMP)

Joshua 1:5-9 No man shall be able to stand before you all the days of your life. As I was with Moses, so I will be with you; I will not fail you or forsake you. Be strong (confident) and of good courage, for you shall cause this people to inherit the land which I swore to their fathers to give them. Only you be strong and very courageous, that you may do according to all the law which Moses My servant commanded you. Turn not from it to the right hand or to the left, that you may prosper wherever you go. This Book of the Law shall not depart out of your mouth, but you shall meditate on it day and night, that you may observe {and} do according to all that is written in it. For then you shall make your way prosperous, and then you shall deal wisely {and} have good success. Have not I commanded you? Be strong, vigorous, and very courageous. Be not afraid, neither be dismayed, for the Lord your God is with you wherever you go (AMP).

1 Samuel 17:45-47 Then said David to the Philistine, You come to me with a sword, and with a spear, and with a shield: but I come to you in the name of the LORD of hosts, the God of the armies of Israel, whom you have defied. This day will the LORD deliver you into my hand; and I will smite you, and take your head from you; and I will give the carcasses of the host of the Philistines this day to the fowls of the air, and to the wild beasts of the earth; that all the earth may know that there is a God in Israel. And all this assembly shall know that the LORD saves not with sword and spear: for the battle is the LORD's, and he will give you into our hands. (AKJV)

Isaiah 54:17 "No weapon formed against you shall prosper, and every tongue which rises against you in judgment you shall condemn. This is the heritage of the servants of the Lord, and their righteousness is from Me," says the Lord. (AKJV)

Joel 3:10 Beat your plowshares into swords and your pruning hooks into spears: let the weak say, I am strong. (AKJV)

John 16:33 I have told you these things, so that in Me you may have [perfect] peace {and} confidence. In the world you have tribulation {and} trials {and} distress {and} frustration; but be of good cheer [take courage; be confident, certain, undaunted]! For I have overcome the world. [I have deprived it of power to harm you and have conquered it for you.] (AMP)

Romans 8:37-39 Yet amid all these things we are more than conquerors {and} gain a surpassing victory through Him Who loved us. For I am persuaded beyond doubt (am sure) that neither death nor life, nor angels nor principalities, nor things impending {and} threatening nor things to come, nor powers, Nor height nor depth, nor anything else in all creation will be able to separate us from the love of God which is in Christ Jesus our Lord. (AMP)

1 Corinthians 15:57 But thanks be to God, who gives us the victory through our Lord Jesus Christ (NKJV).

1 Timothy 6:12 Fight the good fight of the faith; lay hold of the eternal life to which you were summoned and [for which] you confessed the good confession [of faith] before many witnesses. (AMP)

Ephesians 4:22-24 Strip yourselves of your former nature [put off and discard your old unrenewed self] which characterized your previous manner of life and becomes corrupt through lusts {and} desires that spring from delusion; And be constantly renewed in the spirit of your mind [having a fresh mental and spiritual attitude], And put on the new nature (the regenerate self) created in God's image, [Godlike] in true righteousness and holiness. (AMP)

32
Prayer

Ephesians 6:18 Pray at all times (on every occasion, in every season) in the Spirit, with all [manner of] prayer and entreaty. To that end keep alert and watch with strong purpose {and} perseverance, interceding in behalf of all the saints (God's consecrated people). (AMP)

Ephesians 1:15-23 For this reason, because I have heard of your faith in the Lord Jesus and your love toward all the saints (the people of God), I do not cease to give thanks for you, making mention of you in my prayers. [For I always pray to] the God of our Lord Jesus Christ, the Father of glory, that He may grant you a spirit of wisdom and revelation [of insight into mysteries and secrets] in the [deep and intimate] knowledge of Him, By having the eyes of your heart flooded with light, so that you can know {and} understand the hope to which He has called you, and how rich is His glorious inheritance in the saints (His set-apart ones), And [so that you can know and understand] what is the immeasurable {and} unlimited {and} surpassing greatness of His power in {and} for us who believe, as demonstrated in the working of His mighty strength, Which He exerted in Christ when He raised Him from the dead and seated Him at His [own] right hand in the heavenly [places], Far above all rule and authority and power and dominion and every name that is named [above every title that can be conferred], not only in this age {and} in this world, but also in the age {and} the world which are to come. And He has put all things under His feet and has appointed Him the universal and supreme Head of the church [a headship exercised throughout the church], Which is His body, the fullness of Him Who fills all in all [for in that body lives the full measure of Him Who makes everything complete, and Who fills everything everywhere with Himself]. (AMP)

Jeremiah 29:11-13 For I know the thoughts that I think toward you, said the LORD, thoughts of peace, and not of evil, to give you an expected end. Then shall you call on me, and you shall go and pray to me, and I will listen to you. And you shall seek me, and find me, when you shall search for me with all your heart. (AKJV)

James 5:17-18 Elijah was a human being with a nature such as we have [with feelings, affections, and a constitution like ours]; and he prayed earnestly for it not to rain, and no rain fell on the earth for three years and six months. [I Kings 17:1.] And [then] he prayed again and the heavens supplied rain and the land produced its crops [as usual]. [I Kings 18:42-45.] (AMP)

Jude 1:20 But you, beloved, build yourselves up [founded] on your most holy faith [make progress, rise like an edifice higher and higher], praying in the Holy Spirit; (AMP)

Ephesians 6:12-13 For we are not wrestling with flesh and blood [contending only with physical opponents], but against the despotisms, against the powers, against [the master spirits who are] the world rulers of this present darkness, against the spirit forces of wickedness in the heavenly (supernatural) sphere. Therefore put on God's complete armor, that you may be able to resist {and} stand your ground on the evil day [of danger], and, having done all [the crisis demands], to stand [firmly in your place]. (AMP)

33

Final Scriptures

Hebrews 1:14 Are not the angels all ministering spirits (servants) sent out in the service [of God for the assistance] of those who are to inherit salvation? (AMP)

Luke 22:25-27 And he said to them, The kings of the Gentiles exercise lordship over them; and they that exercise authority on them are called benefactors. But you shall not be so: but he that is greatest among you, let him be as the younger; and he that is chief, as he that does serve. For whether is greater, he that sits at meat, or he that serves? is not he that sits at meat? but I am among you as he that serves. (AMP)

John 12:23-26 And Jesus answered them, saying, The hour is come, that the Son of man should be glorified. Truly, truly, I say to you, Except a corn of wheat fall into the ground and die, it stays alone: but if it die, it brings forth much fruit. He that loves his life shall lose it; and he that hates his life in this world shall keep it to life eternal. If any man serve me, let him follow me; and where I am, there shall also my servant be: if any man serve me, him will my Father honor. (AMP)

Romans 8:28-30 We are assured {and} know that [God being a partner in their labor] all things work together {and} are [fitting into a plan] for good to {and} for those who love God and are called according to [His] design {and} purpose. For those whom He foreknew [of whom He was aware and loved beforehand], He also destined from the beginning [foreordaining them] to be molded into the image of His Son [and share inwardly His likeness], that He might become the firstborn among many brethren. And those whom He thus foreordained, He also called; and those whom He called, He also justified (acquitted, made righteous, putting them into right standing with Himself). And those whom He justified, He also glorified [raising them to a heavenly dignity and condition or state of being]. (AMP)

Ephesians 1:4 Even as [in His love] He chose us [actually picked us out for Himself as His own] in Christ before the foundation of the world, that we should be holy (consecrated and set apart for Him) and blameless in His sight, {even} above reproach, before Him in love. (AMP)

Ephesians 1:11-12 In Him we also were made [God's] heritage (portion) {and} we obtained an inheritance; for we had been foreordained (chosen and appointed beforehand) in accordance with His purpose, Who works out everything in agreement with the counsel {and} design of His [own] will, So that we who first hoped in Christ [who first put our confidence in Him have been destined and appointed to] live for the praise of His glory! (AMP)

Ephesians 1:13-14 In Him you also who have heard the Word of Truth, the glad tidings (Gospel) of your salvation, and have believed in {and} adhered to {and} relied on Him, were stamped with the seal of the long-promised Holy Spirit. That [Spirit] is the guarantee of our inheritance [the firstfruits, the pledge and foretaste, the down payment on our heritage], in anticipation of its full redemption {and} our acquiring [complete] possession of it--to the praise of His glory. (AMP)

Ephesians 2:22 In Him [and in fellowship with one another] you yourselves also are being built up [into this structure] with the rest, to form a fixed abode (dwelling place) of God in (by, through) the Spirit. (AMP)

Ephesians 2:1-20 For it is through Him that we both [whether far off or near] now have an introduction (access) by one [Holy] Spirit to the Father [so that we are able to approach Him]. Therefore you are no longer outsiders (exiles, migrants, and aliens, excluded from the rights of citizens), but you now share citizenship with the saints (God's own people, consecrated and set apart for Himself); and you belong to God's [own] household. You are built upon the foundation of the apostles and prophets with Christ Jesus Himself the chief Cornerstone. (AMP)

Ephesians 3:1-6 FOR THIS reason [because I preached that you are thus built up together], I, Paul, [am] the prisoner of Jesus the Christ for the sake {and} on behalf of you Gentiles-- Assuming that you have heard of the stewardship of God's grace (His unmerited favor) that was entrusted to me [to dispense to you] for your benefit, [And] that the mystery (secret) was made known to me {and} I was allowed to comprehend it by direct revelation, as I already briefly wrote you. When you read this you can understand my insight into the mystery of Christ. [This mystery] was never disclosed to human beings in past generations as it has now been revealed to His holy apostles (consecrated messengers) and prophets by the [Holy] Spirit. [It is this:] that the Gentiles are now to be fellow heirs [with the Jews], members of the same body and joint partakers [sharing] in the same divine promise in Christ through [their acceptance of] the glad tidings (the Gospel). (AMP)

Ephesians 3:-17 For this reason [seeing the greatness of this plan by which you are built together in Christ], I bow my knees before the Father {of our Lord Jesus Christ,} For Whom every family in heaven and on earth is named [that Father from Whom all fatherhood takes its title and derives its name]. May He grant you out of the rich treasury of His glory to be strengthened {and}

132

reinforced with mighty power in the inner man by the [Holy] Spirit [Himself indwelling your innermost being and personality]. May Christ through your faith [actually] dwell (settle down, abide, make His permanent home) in your hearts! May you be rooted deep in love {and} founded securely on love, (AMP)

Ephesians 3:21 To Him be glory in the church and in Christ Jesus throughout all generations forever and ever. Amen (so be it). (AMP)

Ephesians 4:4-6 [There is] one body and one Spirit--just as there is also one hope [that belongs] to the calling you received- [There is] one Lord, one faith, one baptism, One God and Father of [us] all, Who is above all [Sovereign over all], pervading all and [living] in [us] all. (AMP)

Ephesians 4:14-15 So then, we may no longer be children, tossed [like ships] to and fro between chance gusts of teaching {and} wavering with every changing wind of doctrine, [the prey of] the cunning {and} cleverness of unscrupulous men, [gamblers engaged] in every shifting form of trickery in inventing errors to mislead. Rather, let our lives lovingly express truth [in all things, speaking truly, dealing truly, living truly]. Enfolded in love, let us grow up in every way {and} in all things into Him Who is the Head, [even] Christ (the Messiah, the Anointed One). (AMP)

Ephesians 5:1-2 THEREFORE BE imitators of God [copy Him {and} follow His example], as well-beloved children [imitate their father]. And walk in love, [esteeming and delighting in one another] as Christ loved us and gave Himself up for us, a slain offering and sacrifice to God [for you, so that it became] a sweet fragrance. (AMP)

Philippians 4:13 I can do all things through Christ who strengthens me. (AMP)

2 Peter 1:3-4 For His divine power has bestowed upon us all things that [are requisite and suited] to life and godliness, through the [full, personal] knowledge of Him Who called us by {and} to His own glory and excellence (virtue). By means of these He has bestowed on us His precious and exceedingly great promises,   so that through them you may escape [by flight] from the moral decay (rottenness and corruption) that is in the world because of covetousness (lust and greed), and become sharers (partakers) of the divine nature. (AMP)

Revelation 5:5 Then one of the elders [of the heavenly Sanhedrin] said to me, Stop weeping! See, the Lion of the tribe of Judah, the Root (Source) of David, has won (has overcome and conquered)! He can open the scroll and break its seven seals! (AMP)

Revelation 22:13 I am the Alpha and the Omega, the First and the Last (the Before all and the End of all). (AMP)

Revelation 22:20-21 He Who gives this warning {and} affirms {and} testifies to these things says, Yes (it is true). [Surely] I am coming quickly (swiftly, speedily). Amen (so let it be)! Yes, come, Lord Jesus! The grace (blessing and favor) of the Lord Jesus {Christ (the Messiah)} be with all the saints (God's holy people, those set apart for God, to be, as it were, exclusively His). Amen (so let it be)! (AMP)

Prayer For Salvation

Heavenly Father, I come to you in the name of Jesus. I pray and ask Jesus to come into my heart and be Lord over my life. I confess that Jesus is Lord, and I believe in my heart that God raised Him from the dead. Forgive me of my sins and make me your child. In Jesus' Name. Amen!

The Blessing Scriptures

Other Publications By Taka Sande

The Discipleship Series

If you really want to enjoy your Christian life, this is the book to read. This book provides basic foundational Christian life principles. It covers topics that include personal devotional life, who is God, what is the Bible, who is Jesus Christ, salvation, faith, baptism, prayer, fellowship, giving and charity. The book ends with a topic on Backsliding! It's a good book not only for a new Christian but for anyone who what to know more about the basics of Christian faith. This series of teachings are also guideline for personal Bible study or home groups.

This book is available on Amazon or you can get more information on It's My Footprint website.

The Little Tough Tips on Marriage

Marriage is supposed to be fun and enjoyable. Every couple can have a fun and enjoyable marriage and they can have this if they are brave enough to pursue the Little Tough Tips on Marriage. This little book will revolutionize your approach to your marriage relationship. It will prepare you to navigate traps that can block the smooth flow of marriage, by reorienting your heart and attitude.

This book is also available on Amazon or you can get more information on It's My Footprint website.

It's My Footprint Newsletter

This is an inspirational newsletter that offers wisdom for life. You can subscribe for free to It's My Footprint Newsletter at www.itsmyfootprint.com.

www.ingramcontent.com/pod-product-compliance
Lightning Source LLC
Chambersburg PA
CBHW061733020426
42331CB00006B/1220